C000148244

Picturing the Mind

A simple model capable to explain the functioning
and dysfunctioning of the human psyche.

Volume 1
Introduction to the Field theory of Human Functioning

By
Gary Edward Gedall

2013 - 2015

Published by

From Words to Worlds,

Lausanne, Switzerland

www.fromwordstoworlds.com

E-Book Edition

ISBN: **2-940535-15-6**

ISBN 13: **978-2-940535-15-6**

About the Author

Gary Edward Gedall is a state registered psychologist, psychotherapist, trained in Ericksonian hypnosis and EMDR.

He has ordinary and master's degrees in Psychology from the Universities of Geneva and Lausanne and an Honours Degree in Management Sciences from Aston University in the UK.

He has lived as an associate member of the Findhorn Spiritual Community, has been a regular visitor to the Osho meditation centre in Puna, India. And as part of his continuing quest into alternative beliefs and healing practices, he completed the three-year practical training, given by the Foundation for Shamanic Studies in 2012.

He is now, (2014 – 2016), studying for a DAS, (Diploma of Advanced Studies), as a therapist using horses.

His hobbies are; writing, western riding and spoiling his children. Quora writer of the year 2015

He is currently living and working in Lausanne, Switzerland.

By the same Author

Adventures with the Master

REMEMBER

Tasty Bites (Series – published or in preproduction)
Face to Face
Free 2 Luv
Heresy
Love you to death
Master of all Masters
Pandora's Box
Shame of a family
The Noble Princess
The Ugly Barren Fruit Tree
The Woman of my Dreams

The Island of Serenity, Pt 1 Destruction

(Series – published or in preproduction)

Book1 :	**The Island of Survival**
Book 2:	**Sun & Rain**
Book 3:	**The Island of Pleasure (Vol 1)**
Book 4:	**The Island of Pleasure (Vol 2)**
Book 5:	**Rise & Fall**
Book 6:	**The Island of Esteem**
Book 7:	**The Faron Show**
Book 8:	**The Island of Love**

(Non Fiction)   **The Zen approach to Low Impact Training and Sports**

Disclaimer:

The characters and events related in my books are a synthesis of all that I have seen and done, the people that I have met and their stories. Hence, there are events and people that have echoes with real people and real events, however no character is taken purely from any one person and is in no way intended to depict any person, living or dead.

My books are not, in any way a therapy books and are not meant to contradict or invalidate, any other vision of the human being or their psyche, nor any particular therapy.

Picturing the Mind

A simple, single model, accessible to everyone, to explain the development, functioning and dis-functioning of the human psyche.

Avant Pro:

For the common man and woman in the street, the complex and competing theories and models of the human psyche; its development, functioning and dis-functioning are often unhelpful for their understanding of themselves.

This becomes even more problematic when they find themselves in difficulty, as often, even the mental health professionals, who are experts in their own fields, find themselves at a loss to communicate successfully how and why the patent is unwell and what needs to happen to find or regain a healthy balance.

This opens up the question; 'is it possible to image a simple, single model, accessible to everyone, to explain the development, functioning and dis-functioning of the human psyche?'

One that builds on existing theories and models, benefitting from the mass of experience and research of 'modern western' psychological concepts and ideas, but also integrating traditional visions of the human psyche and modern theories from the physical sciences.

Picturing the Mind, is an attempt to answer to this need.

Contents

INTRODUCTION: - 1 -

1.   THE TWO MODELS OF REFERENCE: - 4 -

1.1   THE SHAMANIC IMPULSION   - 4 -

1.2   QUANTUM FIELD DYNAMICS: - 4 -

1.3   A SYNTHETIC VIEW: - 5 -

2.   BASIC CONCEPTS AND REFLECTIONS   - 6 -

2.1   THE PIECES OF THE PUZZLE: - 6 -

2.2   THE SHAMANIC IMPULSION   - 6 -

2.3   LIMITATIONS IN USING THE SHAMANIC MODEL: - 8 -

2.4.   LOVE; IN SICKNESS AND IN HEALTH: - 12 -

2.5.   QUANTUM FIELD DYNAMICS: - 17 -

2.6 SIFTABLES: - 23 -

2.7 QUANTUM FIELD SIFTABLES   - 24 -

2.8 .TOWARDS A NEW PARADIGM: - 28 -

3.   RUPERT SHELDRAKE & MORPHIC FIELDS   - 37 -

3.1 THE HYPOTHESIS OF MORPHIC FIELDS   - 37 -

3.2 THE CONVERGENCES AND DIVERGENCES OF THE TWO
MODELS.   - 39 -

4.   FINAL REFLECTIONS ON THIS SECTION   - 41 -

5.   ON THE PSYCHE AND THE SOUL?   - 43 -

5.1 THE PSYCHE OR THE SOUL?   - 43 -

5.2 A NEW VISION   - 45 -

5.3 A NEW TERMINOLOGY?   - 47 -

6.   THE CREATION OF THE HUMAN PSYCHE AND SOUL   - 50 -

6.1 IN THE BEGINNING: - 50 -

6.2   THE SOUL, A VARIABLY DIMENSIONED SPACE: - 51 -

6.3   EARLIEST DEVELOPMENT, THE DIFFERENTIATION OF THE
SOUL: - 52 -

6.4   THE ACTIVATION OF THE PSYCHE: - 54 -

7.   THE BIRTH OF EMOTIONS   - 58 -

7.1   THE QUESTION OF CAUSALITY: - 58 -

7.2   EMOTIONS - A NEW PARADIGM: - 61 -

7.3   THE GENESIS OF EMOTIONS: - 64 -

7.4   ANY ONE OF THREE?   - 68 -

7.5.   EVERYBODY IS RIGHT!   - 70 -

8.   EARLY STAGES   - 72 -

8.1   BIRTH, THE 1ST SEPARATION & MEETINGS   - 72 -

8.2   THE RELATIONSHIP FIELD AND TRANSITIONAL OBJECTS- 75 -

8.3   THE RELATIONSHIP FIELD   - 75 -

9.   TRANSITIONAL OBJECTS – MYTHS AND REALITIES   - 77 -

9.1   WHAT WE THINK WE KNOW: - 77 -

9.2   A MOTHER SUBSTITUTE OR WHAT?   - 80 -

10.   THE GROWTH PROCESS OF THE PSYCHIC ENVELOPE: - 85 -

10.1   FOOD FOR THOUGHT   - 85 -

10.2   THE FIRST LEARNING EXPERIENCES
INTEROCEPTION   - 91 -

10.3   THE FIRST LEARNING EXPERIENCES
EXTEROCEPTION   - 93 -

11.   NEXT STEPS   - 102 -

11.1   FIRST CONSTRUCTS   - 102 -

11.2   EXPLICIT MESSAGES   - 105 -

11.3   IMPLICIT MESSAGES   - 107 -

11.4   ON THE NOURISHING OF THE SOUL AND THE PSYCHIC
ENVELOPE: - 111 -

12 ON THE BUILDING OF THE PSYCHIC MACHINE: - 113 -

12.1 INFORMATIONAL ELEMENTS: - 113 -

12.2   NEUTRAL ELEMENTS   - 114 -

12.3 CHARGED ELEMENTS   - 117 -

13.   THE CONSCIOUS THE UNCONSCIOUS AND THE FORGOTTEN- 120 -

13.1   BASIC CONCEPTS   - 120 -

13.2.1   REACTIONS TO EXPLICIT NEGATIVE FEEDBACK   - 125 -

13.3   REACTIONS TO IMPLICIT NEGATIVE FEEDBACK   - 130 -

13.4   FINAL REFLECTIONS ON THE CONSCIOUS THE
UNCONSCIOUS AND THE FORGOTTEN   - 133 -

14.   WHO AM I?   - 136 -

14.1   WHEN DO I BECOME A WHO?   - 136 -

14.2   HOW OTHERS SEE US: - 139 -

14.3   HOW WE EXPRESS OURSELVES AS A PERSON   - 142 -

14.4   HOW WE SEE OURSELVES   - 144 -

14.5   THE STAGES OF BEING US   - 145 -

14.6   THE IDENTITY FIELD   - 150 -

15.   FINAL THOUGHTS ON VOLUME 1   - 154 -

Introduction:

The mind or the psyche is a horribly complex entity.

A system, more powerful and much more complex than any computer that exists to date.

A system that creates and regulates itself, for the whole of our lives, without hesitation or pause.

However, it is not infallible; far, far from that. It is notably very imprecise and often full of errors. Worse still, its level of functioning is particularly variable and all too often falls. Well below that which it needs to keep the system operating correctly.

In many cases, even the self-regulating and self-repairing mechanisms fail and we find ourselves in the world of mental sickness, which is to say, psycho-pathology.

The soul is if anything, even more challenging to comprehend and to grasp. And yet, these two elements, as many of us understand the 'concept' of a human being, are considered to be the fundamental components of who we are.

In this work; my aim is to try and offer a picture, (not THE picture, not THE truth), of how the psyche and / or the soul (terms to be re-defined below), are formed within the human being, how they function in normal situations and conditions and how we might understand them when the system functions less well and when we experience emotional and psychological pain and suffering.

This is not meant to be a definitive exposition or vulgarisation of the most current theories of human development and psychopathology. Quite the opposite, this is a personal view based on a very wide vision of the human condition, taking into account visions and experiences from many value systems, cultures and eras.

In short, this is my own understanding of how we are, how we've come to be how we are and how this can work reasonably well or not, depending on many competing factors. A lot of this imagery and explanations I use in my regular practice, and I find that it helps my patients to better visualise and understand their situations and conditions.

We are always well aware that these images and explanations are only one particular construct that I am choosing to use; many, many others are just as, if not more legitimate.

However, I feel that these representations are often much easier to understand and to deal with than other, equally valid yet more complex models.

My inspiration to create this work came from two very different models; one, older than anyone can guess and a second, less the one year old, at the time of writing.

1. The two models of reference:

1.1   The Shamanic Impulsion

The shamanic image of how we function and dis-
function comes, not from the psyche, (which does not
exist in their system), but from the soul; both whole
and healthy or with parts lacking and / or contaminated
from outside sources. The shamans' two main healing
functions are; to retrieve lost parts of the soul or to
extract evil and poisonous energies from it.

1.2   Quantum Field Dynamics:

Quantum field theory, postulates that all matter is made
up particles or properties, held together by an energy
force, a field. Neither the particles, (properties), nor the
field are fixed nor invariable, they can vary depending
on many interacting factures.

1.3   A synthetic view:

Although, at first sight, these two visions have nothing in common, combining their concepts and incorporating nearly a hundred years of theories about the development and functioning of humans, on both the individual and group levels, a holistic, yet relatively simple model of the human 'psyche' can be elaborated.

This model encompasses such diverse themes as; prenatal experiences and the bases of emotional and hormonal functioning, very early learning experiences, (values, norms and vetoes), normal and none-normal development, the conscious and the unconscious, remembering and forgetting, emotional investment, lack and loss, creativity, personal, intimate, social and group relationships, as well as, intuition and deep mental processes.

In short, this model is capable to explain, in fairly simple and visual terms, all the functioning and dis-functioning of the human psyche.

I hope and trust that you will find it interesting, illuminating and thought provoking.

Gary Edward Gedall

2. Basic Concepts and Reflections

2.1 The pieces of the puzzle:

As I have mentioned in the introduction, the two main concepts that have led me to this model have been that of shamanism and of quantum field theory. I will now elaborate on the basic tenants of these two heteroclite models of the human, (and none-human) systems.

2.2 The Shamanic Impulsion

The initial impulse to write this book came from the shamanic image of man.

In its most simplified form, in their tradition, due to some form of trauma or theft, parts of the soul can separate themselves from the whole never to return unaided.

On the other side of the story; one can fairly easily 'catch' an evil spirit, (as one might catch a cold), or, just as likely, an enemy or rival could send you negative energy, which might range from the simply disagreeable up to the positively fatal.

Hence the shamans' two main healing functions are; to retrieve lost parts of the soul or to extract evil and poisonous energies from it.

Having undertaken a training of 'shamanic practitioner' with the Federation for Shamanic Studies, (FSS), and having the opportunity to have a personal interview on the subject with a native shaman Ricardo Tsakimp*, I felt legitimate to introduce these concepts and images into my psychotherapeutic practice.

And even though I would never think to practice shamanism per se on my patients, (I keep certain boundaries between my various interests and practices), these concepts and images have proven their just value.

*Ricardo Tsakimp is Uwishin, which means "shaman" in Shuar language. Is the founder of the Association of the Shuar shamans. He has worked several years in the Department of Intercultural Health Provinciale (DPSI) and continues to work with the Department of Traditional Medecine Shuar in Sucua
.

2.3   Limitations in using the Shamanic Model:

However, I quite soon found the simple concept of a, (I suppose), pure, solid, white fixed sized, sphere, (my own representation of course), punctured with gaps due to 'soul loss' but with ugly intrusions due to some form of contamination, much too simplistic to represent all that I considered that happens to the human psyche.

– Yes, I am very aware that I have segued from soul to psyche but it is just this change of focus or definition which opens wide the gates to further development of the concept.

As noted above; for many native tribes, the concept of the psyche doesn't exist, while for the purest scientific, neither does the soul. If we choose to accept that there is a part of all living creatures that is beyond the physical entity of the brain. To name it as soul or psyche or mind, could be considered as little more than a question of language.

Although I'm sure many philosophers and religious, would strongly debate this position.

However, for the purposes of this reflection, I choose work with the two concepts

So, if I was to use this model as a basis, I would have to open up the image to include the following concepts; birth, maturation & evolution, the acquisition of knowledge, behaviours, & attitudes, the functioning of the emotions & all related the hormonal interactions, also the links to the physical experiencing of the human body.

I would also have to integrate all the different emotional states; comfort, hope, love, satisfaction, happiness, optimism. As well as loss, hurt, anger, deception, depression, discomfort, to name just some of the list.

Within these states and experiences, I would suppose that the size of the thing would more vary, then stay the same.

Also, the losing of parts of the soul / psyche would be variable, with the possibility of a natural form of 'soul retrieval'.

As with the concept of contamination. The system would have to be able to cleanse itself from most types of contaminations.

However, as with the difference of opinion that many have with the psycho-analytic vision of the unconscious that stocks itself only with repressed thoughts and impulses.

As compared with the Ericksonian, (Milton Erickson), vision is that there is also stocked many hidden and lost resources.

Likewise, in the traditional point of view, (from what I understand), energy coming in is a dangerous contamination.

Which, in no way can take into account positive, supportive and loving energy that we have all, (I hope), experienced at some time from someone.

And on the angle of psychological and psychiatric disorders, they would then be linked with:

A disturbed development of the system,

With the inability to cope with usual types and situations of soul loss,

With the inability to re-integrate soul elements that need to be re-integrated,

With the inability to cope with a usual level of contamination,

With the inability to cleanse oneself appropriately of contamination.

This list of disorders might seem difficult to accept and / or understand, so I will use an everyday example, to explain and expand my reflection.

2.4. Love; in Sickness and in Health:

If one was to think of the two situations in which we could experience a state that might be considered as 'soul loss' as a consequence of normal, everyday life, the two states which immediately came to mind are; being in love and being in hate.

Taking the situation the most written of in all literature, I will chose, to describe the state of 'being in love'.

The more one is taken by the experience of being in love, the more one is dysfunctional in all areas of one's normal, daily life; one cannot concentrate, eat, sleep or keep any thought not linked with the 'bien aimé', (the loved one), in one's conscience for more than five minutes at a time.

One flips between the feelings of warmth, tenderness and deepest well-being, to equally deep feelings of loneliness, emptiness and despair, ('You always feel lonely, when you're in love'), but what is clearly evident, is that the person as we have known them – is no longer totally there.

To return to the classical shamanic concepts, we could definitely imagine that his or her soul has been 'captured' by the other.

(An image or concept used in poetry, music and literature since time immemorial).

However, looking at these 'symptoms' from a psychiatric point of view; concentration difficulties, perturbations in the areas of eating and sleeping, invasive thoughts, lack of motivation for usual occupations and important moods swings, often towards the negative, we have a clear diagnosis for depression.

(If one would care to add, moments of euphoria, we could even defend a diagnosis of manic-depressive or bi-polar disorder.)

Which is very much the position of Sandra Ingleman, who links, in her seminal book, 'Soul Recovery'*, (based on much personal work and experience), soul loss, with depressive symptoms.

*Soul Retrieval: Mending the Fragmented Self Paperback – : HarperOne; August 8, 2006, ISBN-13: 978-0061227868   www.sandraingerman.com

We now start to find some sort of coherent vision or understanding of a phenomenon.

Due to a particular set of circumstances, when a large part of the human psyche is not available in its usual way, we find a constellation of effects which fit into a pattern, diagnosed in the west as depression.

Using the same logic, but now looking at the occurrence of a crisis of anger, we notice that we find the same assemblage of signs.

In fact, any major emotional state brings about the same package of reactions, be it; anxiety, positive expectations, worry, fears etc...

To label each and every one of these emotion states as depression is of course a nonsense, but to group all of these states under a general concept does make sense.

By the same reflection, but from the shamanic point of view, to look at all these instances as a form of unhealthy, 'soul loss', for which a journey of soul retrieval might well be necessary, is also unreasonable.

As with most things in life, what seems to me to be important is to be able to understand what is happening; to then have a means to assess if this experience fits into something that we can consider as normal or not.

If it is normal but on some level disturbing, then to undertake the necessary measures to relieve as much suffering as possible until it completes its own cycle and if it is not normal, in some way or ways, then to know how to deal with this as a problem.

One classic theme in Science Fiction stories is when an alien creature suddenly starts to transform or exhibit very strange behaviours; which the humans read as some sort of awful sickness or disease.

They then try to cure the creature of its sickness, but only to subsequently discover that what has happened as a totally natural process for the alien.

(I have also used this concept in one of my 'Peter the Pixie', stories – 'Transformation').

It often seems to me, that many of my patients are not aware that they are experiencing phenomena which are fundamentally normal and healthy but are not within their known or acceptable range of experiences.

Being so strongly affected by an emotional relationship to someone or something, that we cease to function normally, is not a sickness; it is part of the human condition. When it starts to adversely affect our daily lives, only then should we consider intervening.

Hence a model that can accommodate these experience becomes necessary.

To further open the reflection of how (soul / psychic) elements might exist within unique 'spaces' and to set the scene for the discussions on how the psyche is formed and functions, we shall now look into the latest thinking on the most fundamental aspects of how the world operates.

2.5.   Quantum Field Dynamics:

In the August 2013 edition of Scientific American, (pp32-39), in his article, 'what is real?', the author Meinard Kuhlmann, postulates a new, refined view of how the world is constructed / organised.

He takes the classical model of 'particle physics', in which all things are constructed from a number of particles held together by an energy field, (the most general images of this being the atom and our solar system), and expands it, to take into account new research findings and theories.

He argues that particles are not permanent entities, existing in a fixed space and that the energy that binds them together operates more as a series of functions, which then operate on the particles to come to a 'value'.

However, in quantum field theory, there is a final step in which one must apply the operator to another mathematical entity, known as a 'state vector'. The state vector is a holistic entity as it describes the system as a whole.

If I have lost you here, take heart, it is, after all, Quantum Dynamics that we are talking about here.

To try and simplify this a bit:

Everything that exists is made of groups of things, from the whole universe with its multitude of stars and planets, down to the smallest entities known to man.

Every group is held together in its specific configuration by some type of energy field, which keeps the components together, with its specific properties; electric, magnetic, mass, etc.

What Meinard Kuhlmann is suggesting is that each energy field does NOT follow a fixed, permanent 'pattern', nor do all the elements always stay the same, but all can change, following a much more complex set of rules.

He continues to reflect that; 'We may never know the real natures of things but only how they are related to one another.

Take the example of mass.

Do you ever see mass itself?

No. You see only what it means for other entities or, concretely, how one massive body is related to another massive body through the local gravitational field.

The structure of the world, reflecting how things are interrelated, is the most enduring part of physics theories.

New theories may overturn our conception of the basic building blocks of the world, but they tend to preserve the structures.'

- The structures being, how the objects interact with each other.

'....examples of structures that take priority over their material realization are the World Wide Web, the brain's neural network and the genome.

All of them still function even when individual computers, cells, atoms and people die.

These examples are loose analogies, although they are close in spirit to the technical arguments that apply to quantum field theory.'

He turns his attention, (I trust that yours is still holding on), to what he refers to as 'properties'. Properties, are the different elements that make up an object.

For instance, colour, weight, size, texture, solidity …

'Traditionally, people assume that properties are "universals"— in other words, they belong to an abstract, general category.

They are always possessed by particular things; they cannot exist independently. For instance, when you think of red, you usually think of particular red things and not of some freely floating item called "redness."

But you could invert this way of thinking. You can regard properties as having an existence, independently of objects that possess them. Properties may be what philosophers call "particulars"—concrete, individual entities.

What we commonly call a thing may be just a bundle of properties: colour, shape, consistency, and so on.

Construing things as bundles of properties is not how we usually conceptualize the world, but it becomes less mysterious if we try to unlearn how we usually think about the world and set ourselves back to the very first years of life.

As infants, when we see and experience a ball for the first time, we do not actually perceive a ball, strictly speaking.

What we perceive is a round shape, some shade of red, with a certain elastic touch. Only later we do associate this bundle of perceptions with a coherent object of a certain kind—namely, a ball.

Next time we see a ball, we essentially say, "Look, a ball," and forget how much conceptual apparatus is involved in this seemingly immediate perception.

Out there in the world, things are nothing but bundles of properties. It is not that we first have a ball and then attach properties to it. Rather we have properties and call it a ball.

There is nothing to a ball but its properties.

In an attempt to synthesise these ideas into two basic concepts, I would suggest:

Firstly; particles are not simple fixed entities, but can appear different, in different places, at different times and in different circumstances. These particles are brought / held together by an energy / field which can also vary due to many complex factors.

Secondly; what we perceive as things, are nothing more than a bundle of properties: colour, shape, consistency, and so on.

To join the two concepts together; we can further refine the model into one where:

Everything that we perceive, experience or express, are, in fact, only specific combinations of a number of particles, that each exhibit a particular facet, in this specific moment, brought and held together by one or many energy fields, defined in this said moment, uniquely for this purpose.

2.6 Siftables:

David Merill and his team have created a very interesting invention that, in some ways, work in a similar fashion to the concepts outlined above. They have created individual, (computer), blocks, that look like simple two inch screens.

However, these blocks have the capacity to interact with each other, just though being in physical contact; therefore displaying different qualities, (the screens change colour or display another symbol), depending on which other siftables, they are interacting with. And which program they are running.

In a fashion, they create mini energy fields that influence how the individual blocks react and look.

[*Siftables: Towards Sensor Network User Interfaces In Proceedings of the 1st International Conference on Tangible and Embedded Interaction (2007), pp. 75-78, doi:10.1145/1226969.1226984 [http://dl.acm.org/citation.cfm?doid=1226969.1226984] by David Merrill, Jeevan Kalanithi, Pattie Maes]*

2.7 Quantum Field Siftables

By linking the two last sections together, one arrives at the following.

The universe, on both the micro and macro levels exists following the following Maxims:

- Every experience that we have, every object or thing is 'only' a specific grouping of particles.

- Particles come and are held together in various fields.

- The size, shape structure and strength of the field varies at any given time. Hence they can be momentary, transitory, temporary, short-lived, accepted, invested, or even, more or less permanent.

- The particles are interdependent, the proximity of any one or group of particles can influence the expression of other particles that are attracted into the field.

- A group of particles in any field creates a construct.

- By changing the shape or form or the removal of an important particle, or by introducing new particles the other particles can change, hence changing the construct.

- A construct is anything that can be made up of particles; physical objects, but also ideas and emotions.

- Fields hold themselves and the particles in the form of constructs by a series of forces; magnetic, gravitational, electro-magnetic, physical, but also through social, political, relational, financial, military, intellectual and emotional means.

- Fields are construct specific, which means to say that each different construct creates a different field. The more they continue similar elements, (particles), the more they will operate in the same space, time dimension.

- Different fields have different parameters, hence different time, space constraints; field of vision, hearing, or, of course, the physical body.

- Energy from different fields, (people etc.,), are not restricted by fields generated by others, unless there is a barrier that restricts that exact emission. (A pair of headphones will block out sound, but not light).

- Energy from people and things can pass into other people and things.

- Constructs can be, and often are, 'multi-layered', integrating smaller and smaller constructs, which act as particles within the larger construct.

- Constructs when acting as particles within a larger construct, still have the ability to influence other constructs of the same level, as with all particles.

- A particle can belong to an infinite number of constructs at any one time. Although the energy available is not unlimited.

- A particle can display different facets in different groups, depending on the constellation or influence of other particles within those different groups.

- The range of different facets is however relatively limited as it is likely to be itself a construct of more fundamental particles

- If there is an important change in a particle, that change is likely to be reflected in most, if not all groups, (constructs), that it is integrated into.

2.8. Towards a new paradigm:

By merging the most traditional and the most modern theories of the universe, we find ourselves with a very interesting new vision.

One could choose to view the soul / psyche as a mass of particles, blocks, and constructs.

Clearly, these entities need to be further defined:

Particles of information, (physical, mental, emotional or other), either enter into our psychic space or are created by us.

Blocks; refer to a number of particles that are linked together, (often because they were experienced by the person in the same moment of time), thus creating a form of semi-permanent field

Both particles and constructs can be energetically, emotional neutral or not.

Constructs; are groupings of blocks, which join together, in any one moment, to create a structure, which is contained within an energy field.

Every moment of our lives, through all our senses, (including dream experiences, shamanic journeys, guided meditations, drug trips and psychotic episodes, etc.), we capture or create these particles, and blocks. At this point they might well be energetically and emotionally neutral.

However, as soon as they might become associated with a physical and / or emotion experience, or are attracted into an existing energised field, they transform into energised particles or blocks.

These particles or blocks are combined into constructs, which are held together by various types of fields. Which, in the logic of Quantum Dynamics, can be created, re-created changed or dissolved in any given moment.

There are two basic categories of fields; **energised fields** that contain energised particles, blocks and constructs and **energetically neutral fields** that function with non-energised particles or neutral constructs.

By looking at how we might react to two toys we can see how these two types of fields function.

A fluffy teddy bear can evoke feelings of safety and security, by linking various blocks or particles to a construct, containing experiences where warmth soothing and affection are found. (Similar to those elements that make up a transitional object).

Where-as the combined properties of round, soft and bouncing when brought together, via a field that becomes a 'ball field', creates the perception of a ball but without (necessarily), any specific personal reaction.

The possibility that these elements (particles or constructs – energised or not)), can vary in their properties from one moment to the next, and combine and re-combine ad infinitum, is essential in understanding of how we can generate an almost infinite number of thoughts and associations from any one stimulus.

However, if we then expand this concept, removing any idea of physical or geographical limitation, we can include particles and fields that span time and distance.

Which is to say; that energised particles or constructs, which are created within the psychic space of a person, can become part of a field outside of that person; linked to another person, a group or even a project.

There then becomes the possibility for a part of ourselves to be very strongly linked to something, another construct outside of ourselves.

In this case, the importance of the attraction of the other makes it difficult, if not impossible, for that construct, and the elements that make it up to still be available to be used elsewhere, internally or within other meta-constructs.

It is at this point that we now find an echo in the traditional / shamanic view of a person.

By accepting that part of their soul, (psyche), as much as that part, (or to be more exact, combination of particles / constructs), might, for some reason, no longer be available to combine with other parts of our psyche, we can experience this as lack, as loss of soul.

However, I would go much further with this reflection; I feel that every encounter can create a field or energetic link, in which certain groups of energised particles or soul fragments can become joined to a field linked to the other person(s) or thing.

To further simplify the image, one might prefer to imagine that parts of the psyche actually pass from one person to another person, or object or idea.

Or they might, with elements from others, create a new field, where the particles exist in an intermediary space.

(One needs not to forget that even objects and ideas own their own form of energy fields).

Whether our energies enter into the other, (person or project), or that between ourselves and the other, we create a shared energy field, in which those particles become lodged; or a combination depends on the situation and the protagonists.

What is fundamental to the model, is that the limit of what we consider as 'ourselves' is only one field amongst many others, can be termed as the soul or psychic envelope.

Within that field we have the three important meta fields; the conscious, unconscious and the forgotten, and within those are many, many other fields and sub fields, constantly overlapping, forming and reforming.

However, outside of the psychic envelope we have a whole world of other fields; family, extended family and close friends, neighbours, work and school, religious groups, village or suburb, town, city, state and country.

Added to that are all the things, thoughts, projects and events: 'past, present and future', which either, like pets and plants have their own 'life force' or, as with dreams and desires, have energy projected into them by the person, and or other people.

So, every person or thing that we contact, on any level, generates a field with or between us. Into that energy field, certain quantities of constructions or simple particles are attracted both from ourselves and the 'other'.

Depending on the interest and importance of that which we have contacted, more or less matter will be invested, as well as the strength and resistance of the field.

The stronger this field is, the more our constructs are linked to the elements in that field, hence they become less accessible to other fields, both within our own 'selves' or to other, competing external fields.

Which is to say, throughout our lives we make hundreds of thousands if not millions of contacts and fields.

However, not every contact is of the same importance; my relationship with the person that serves me coffee on the way to work each day is much less important than with my boss or parent or spouse.

So, in fact, some contact fields are weak while others are strong. Hence, important contacts create large, powerful fields that attract many parts of our psyches (or souls) that can have an important effect on our capacity to function and how we experience our daily lives.

On a different, related subject, one might inquire; 'why do I also include events: 'past, present and future'? '

Just ask any teacher how they feel about teaching the last periods on a Friday afternoon, most of them will complain that half the class has already 'left' for the week-end, even if the classroom is still full of students.

The students have projected parts of themselves into the future; hence they are much less present in the classroom.

When we have had or are going to have an important meeting with someone, then we either; replay and replay the past incident over and over again, sometimes with slight variations or we image how the future exchange might be.

And of course, in the situations discussed above; when our focus, strongly positive or negative lands on a person, we link ourselves to that person, so much so that it is often, almost impossible to grab it back.

How many people, before the advent of portable phones, wasted hours and hours just sitting, waiting, hoping that a certain person would ring or even before then, waiting daily for the postman to see if someone has written?

So, we have come, more or less full circle, however, just to prove that thoughts and ideas pass through many channels, it is important to look at the break through ideas and work of Rupert Sheldrake.

3. Rupert Sheldrake & Morphic Fields

Rupert Sheldrake in his best selling book '*A New Science of Life: The Hypothesis of Morphic Resonance*', 1981, now in its 3rd edition (**2009**), outlined, what was then, an entirely new concept; Morphic fields.

This description is taken from the IONS net site, (see link below)
-

3.1 The Hypothesis of Morphic Fields

"All self-organizing systems are wholes made up of parts, which are themselves wholes at a lower level, such as atoms in molecules and molecules in crystals.

The same is true of organelles in cells, cells in tissues, tissues in organs, organs in organisms, organisms in social groups. At each level, the morphic field gives each whole its characteristic properties and interconnects and coordinates the constituent parts.

The fields responsible for the development and maintenance of bodily form in plants and animals are called morphogenetic fields

In animals, the organization of behavior and mental activity depends on behavioral and mental fields. The organization of societies and cultures depends on social and cultural fields. All these kinds of organizing fields are morphic fields.

Morphic fields are located within and around the systems they organize. Like quantum fields, they work probabilistically.

They restrict, or impose order upon, the inherent indeterminism of the systems under their influence.

Social fields coordinate the behavior of individuals within social groups, for example, the behavior of fish in schools or birds in flocks."

3.2   The convergences and divergences of the two models.

There are clearly many similarities between the concepts of morphogenetic and morphic fields and the energy fields which I refer to, and there are a number of areas where the two meet.

Many of the ideas relating to the communication from one animal / person to another, using means that as yet we can neither perceive nor identify are common to both. (More of this will be discussed in later chapters).

As is the idea that we are made up from a variety of different fields, which have different properties and are not limited in time and space. The analogy with light and sound waves is a helpful image.

However, as I understand it, the morphogenetic fields; although allowing for the possibility of change, inherent within the model, change is relatively slow, limited and unidirectional.

The fields in our model, although there must also be some form of basic structural pattern that they respond to, are much, much more mobile in their construction.

Also can change and reform in a totally, almost limitless fashion.

Also, Sheldrake's work is based on his scientific training in biology and biochemistry. Which, although transmuted in later years, with his links to spirituality is still primarily focused on animal and plant systems.

As my background is that of a psychologist, (but also with an interest for spirituality), the focus of this work is much more directed towards an understanding of human systems and on the creation and functioning of the human psyche.

I will also re-iterate that I am neither trying to re-invent the wheel, nor to propose that this image nor interpretation of the psyche is the true or only valid model.

http://www.noetic.org/noetic/issue-four-november-2010/morphic-fields-and-morphic-resonance/

4. Final reflections on this section

It seems reasonable to accept the following ideas:

That there are many types of fields, which function on all levels of existence, from the smallest sub-atomic groupings, through to solar systems and galaxies.

That these fields can create and or structure within themselves certain groupings, which have a sense or function.

That these groupings are not fixed and can change or evolve over time, due to certain circumstances.

That the concept of the human psyche can be imagined as made up of a series of fields. And that these fields might have access to an enormous mass of particles & / or constructs, which can change 'states' at any moment and can be grouped and regrouped in any number of combinations and permutations.

That by expanding the 'traditional' view of the human soul, (or psyche), that it is reasonable to accept the representation of a natural process where individuals can link or deposit parts of ourselves in others.

That 'others' can also include things or concepts.

That it is also interesting to imagine that these parts of people can also be released into an intermediate space, which creates a new shared field.

Having come to accept the possibility to vision the human environment in these terms, this has excited my imagination and my desire to further investigate the ramifications if one should visualise the human mind, in these terms.

It is from there, that other ideas have appeared and been developed and hence this work has come into form.

5. On the Psyche and the Soul?

5.1 The Psyche or the Soul?

In my introduction, I have first spoken of the soul in relation to the shamanic traditional view of the human being, I then, intentionally, slipped into using the term, psyche.

In fact neither term is sufficient in itself to express and encompass the globality of the workings of how humans, (and maybe animals), function.

The term psyche, synonym for many, of the mind; deals with learning, thinking, conscious memory and directed behaviours.

The soul, (also, for many); is a nebulous, eternal entity which, although intrinsically linked with our physical forms, has little or no interaction with our daily lives nor can influence or be influenced by it.

To complicate matters even further in certain belief systems we have 5 unique 'bodies' or layers, (for some others we have 7), which make up the human being.

- This has nothing to do with the chakras, which is part of a different conceptual system.

If this subject interests you, a very informative site on this subject can be found at; www.agoyangyang.com/content.php?id=85 5/5

In my own experiences, I have mostly come across the 5 representations of the 'parts' of the human; physical, emotional, mental, etheric (or energetic) and spiritual, which have up until worked well for me.

Well, up until now

5.2   A new vision

What I now feel to be true is that all living creatures are a synergetic functioning of all of these dimensions.

And to truly understand ourselves; how we function and how we dysfunction, all of these qualities have to be seen as interlocking and interacting elements, as parts of a greater whole.

A concept of the 5 bodies as I have listed above works well enough, what in practice I feel to be lacking is a more integrated vision.

What we often see in psychotherapy is a very clear contamination of the mental functioning by the emotional body. The continual explanations of our acts, stemming from our emotional needs through mental rationalisations is daily fodder for most therapists.

Also, for instance we regularly come across the question; 'what is depression and why does it succeed to sap all the physical, mental and emotional energy from the patient?'

Using the 5 bodies schema; does that mean that it is really only the energetic body that is sick and hence it cannot continue to serve its primary purpose of supplying energy to the system?

But is the energetic body not itself, to some degree nourished by the soul?

Or is it quite the other way around and the energetic body is only the expression of the functioning of the other 'lower' three bodies?

From my experience, and in my vision of today, I reiterate, all parts must by interconnected and interdependent.

5.3   A new terminology?

Very often when a writer imagines a new paradigm, his, (her), first reaction is to start to imagine 'new' words or terms, (often borrowed from Greek or Latin), to express these new ideas.

I personally tend to find this approach, (although of course, totally valid), often confusing and therefore difficult to follow.

Hence, in the search for simplicity and ease of understanding, I have decided on the following formula;

I shall not introduce any new words to express my concepts, but shall continue to use the two terms, psyche and soul to denote the two complementary facets of this 'new' entity.

However, they will still need to be re-defined so as one can understand how they might satisfy the functions that I see them fulfilling.

The Psyche: This denotes the facet of structure; of learning, of logic, of memory and of mind.

It also links to the emotions, the unconscious and certain elements of the physical body.

One could image this function in terms of masculine, (left brain).

Or from the Chinese philosophical point of view the Yang energy.

The Kabbalistic representation of this would by denoted by Chokmah.

The Soul: This denotes the facet of movement and of energy; it is more interlinked to the spiritual and emotional bodies but also exchanges energy and force with the physical body, (right brain).

This would be the female counterpart, the Ying dimension or Binah.

Creativity can only occur when the psyche and the soul function together bringing movement to structure.

In Western occultism, Binah is seen to take the raw force of Chokmah, and to channel it into the various forms of creation.

Whether this choice will serve to help or to hinder you, my gentle reader, only time and your feedback will tell.

6. The creation of the human psyche and soul

6.1 In the beginning:

In the beginning we have nothing, then we have something, then we have a living being, but from where does the basic life force, spirit, soul, psyche come from?

The answer, of course, lies in your own belief system.

However, one interesting and quite beautiful idea could be that the genesis of the baby's psyche and soul is born out of a thought form created in the mother's own soul.

Where the grain of sand that makes the pearl originates from; the father, the Holy Spirit, a contact with an un-incarnated spirit or 'soul', (in the traditional sense of the term) is a matter of conjecture. - In short, again, your belief system.

However, allowing for the idea, that not-with-standing exactly how or where the spark originates from, it is nurtured within the body and soul of the mother, then, for a long moment, the two entities totally share the mother's soul and psychic space.

6.2   The Soul, a variably dimensioned space:

As opposed to the traditional, shamanic image of the soul, being of a fixed size, our vision encompasses a constantly varying entity. (As described in the Quantum Field section).

As we dream, create, love or hate, our soul reacts and grows.

 One could relate this to what some people call the energy body the etheric body or the aura, as many psychics and disciples of Kirlain photography; claim to be able to see.

On the other side of the coin; sadness, fear, anguish and despair, shrink the soul, often leaving very little space to exist. – I will discuss more on a pathological view of the soul and its (mal) functioning, in a later publication.

As stated, any form of creativity expends the soul, during that process; what happens to this particular energetic mass, depends on what it is and why it exists.

6.3 Earliest development, the differentiation of the soul:

One can well image that the symbiotic relationship of a mother and her growing baby, creates a positive, circular process.

One could well argue that some future mothers do not have positive 'dreams', of their unborn off-springs, so how does this fit into the model?

I would argue that there exists in everyone, the 'dream' of a child; the conscious, intentional, positive or negative reactions only add or subtract from that primordial need to reproduce.

Surely, both the sperm and the egg carry with them energy from both parents, and the real involvement, (or not), of those people and / or animals, present during the pregnancy will also supply energetic input.

The mother dreams / fantasises of her unborn child, this creates a space which fills itself up with psychic and soul energy, the new being contacts this source and at some point, will differentiate part of it as linked to itself.

This subtle contact re-enforces the mother's dream and the energy grows, the little one continues to differentiate parts of whole but there is not yet any separation.

As this energetic mass continues to expand; in parallel, the physical vehicle of the baby is developing and some type of basic psychic and soul stuff is being created.

Parts of this evolving psychic and soul stuff, flow between the mother and child, mixing in with that of the mother, which is then enriched and refined by the process.

Little by little; some of this material finds its 'permanent' home in the baby and the differentiation becomes more marked.

However, the links and the exchanges not only continue but found the basis of all future relationship and most learning experiences.

At this point, when enough of the energetic substance becomes relatively fixed within the physical form, one could deem that the body has a soul.

From the field theory point of view; one would describe this as the moment that the first, discrete energy field is formed.

On a spiritual and psychological level, it the very first instance of the existence of 'I'.

Which then prompts the question; 'at what point can one imagine that a baby has a psyche?

6.4   The Activation of the Psyche:

If one realises that at 24 weeks of growth, an embryo is capable to survive, (with a great deal of medical help of course), one could suggest that this is the point in which it is basically complete, but a baby is capable to hear and to react to sounds from only 18 weeks old.

Yes, to react but in what way? In some studies they have noticed that sound of the mother's voice has a calming effect on the unborn baby.

According to Sophie Scott, professor and expert in speech perception at University College London, in an interview with the BBC,

"We know that babies can hear their mother's voice in the womb and pick up on the pitch and rhythm. New-born babies are soothed by their mother's voice from the minute they are born."

This positive reaction, has to come from somewhere, it has to be learnt, but how, from where, by what mechanism?

I would suggest that we benefit from the model of a computer system. When we switch on a computer for the first time, we active two systems; firstly the 'hard-wired' functions, which bring the system to life and create the possibility for certain basic information to be accessed, in this case the 'boot sector' of the hard drive.

This then reads and acts on a very low level form of 'software', which in turn accesses more and more information, until the system is functioning correctly, (we hope!), when it will be ready for us to enter the specific information and utilities that we wish the computer to function with.

I believe that the baby, as well as all the basic physical functions, must also have a simple 'comfort-discomfort' feedback system.

Being physically, emotionally and energetically linked to the mother, everything that the mother experiences, on some level, the baby experiences too.

At this time one could imagine that the baby is only experiencing through the mother but as it can hear and react to what it hears from 18 weeks old, the baby is, in fact learning how to react to audible stimuli.

It hears something; the mother reacts in a certain fashion, the baby integrates the experience and the next time it hears the same thing, in the same circumstances, it then reacts the same way.

One could say that the baby is coding itself, based on the mother's model code.

Also, the fact that the baby reacts, proves that the psychic functions are sufficiently linked to the babies physical body to create directed, even intentional reactions.

Does this seem a little far-fetched? Not in my own personal experience as when my wife was pregnant with our daughter.

The situation was this; we lived in a studio apartment but had also rented a small room upstairs in the same building.

My wife was on bed rest from the middle of her pregnancy, so when I came home from University, (I was studying psychology at the time), she would be rather pleased when I came in.

As soon as I started to say something, my daughter would give a kick, she reacted to my voice. She was clearly reacting to the positive emotions that my wife was feeling on my return, (comfort).

However, if I went upstairs for an hour to work on the computer, when I came back downstairs again, there was no reaction to my starting to speak.

She could not feel the excitement felt by my wife because my returning from upstairs was not for her, (my wife), an important event, (hence, neither comfort nor discomfort, for my daughter, therefore no reaction).

However, straight after the birth, my wife, (not surprisingly), was rather exhausted but our daughter was too excited to sleep, so it was my voice that calmed her down and put her to sleep.

And, just as the physical baby is born and then separates from but needs to keep contact with the mother's body, at the point that it is only ready and capable to cope with that level of independent functioning.

In same way, the embryonic psyche and soul also partially separates from the mother's. Also as on the physical level, the baby still needs to continue to be nourished as it cannot yet survive alone.

7. The Birth of Emotions

7.1 The question of causality:

One of the questions, most asked in psychological reflections, but not yet convincingly answered, is;

'What creates our emotions'?

The problem stems from this, emotions are a combination of; the reaction to a stimulus, (usually external, but also, often internal), a physical body reaction, the release and reaction to hormones and neurotransmitters and the subjective experience, that itself is referred to as an emotion.

Wikipedia introduces its entry on emotions by reflecting that; 'Emotion is often associated and considered reciprocally influential with mood, temperament, personality, disposition, and motivation, as well as influenced by hormones and neurotransmitters such as dopamine, noradrenaline, serotonin, oxytocin, cortisol and GABA.'

The classic explanation of how an emotional reaction is created works something like this;

I see a snake, from my memory, the image of the snake invokes a fear reaction, the fear reaction stimulates the creation of noradrenaline, which in turn produces adrenaline, the adrenaline then activates the body to react by increasing heart rate, breathing, etc.

And so the person is then in the appropriate state for either 'flight or fight', which will ensure the best possibility of survival.

Although this model is very elegant and makes sense in this particular instance, what it cannot explain is the situation where, for whatever physiological reason, the heart begins to accelerate.

This acceleration, (tachycardia), induces the breath to speed up, the person begins to experience, (in total absence of any other stimulus), the feelings of fear or panic, this, in turn, activates the release of noradrenaline, which in turn produces adrenaline, which then re-enforces the somatic reactions and the subjective experiences of panic or fear.

In fact, as each reaction; physical, emotional or hormonal, can trigger both the others, it is clearly impossible to establish exactly which one is the instigator of the process.

And, even more problematic than that, where to introduce the, (internal or external), stimulus.

7.2 Emotions - A new paradigm:

As I have related, an unborn baby is capable to be aware of happenings outside of the womb and to experience reactions which we are capable the register.

My daughter was aware while I returned to the apartment after being away all day, and expressed her 'joy', (or so we wished to read her reaction), through a series of kicks, as I entered into the room.

One might be tempted to understand this using the classic model, where my presence created a positive stimulus, and her reaction was the kick.

However, this misses out somewhat on any explanation of just how she might have created in her mind, the idea that I was something positive.

Also, the fact that if I went out, to go and study in the room upstairs, when I would come back down, even some several hours later, she would not react to my voice.

How comes, for the same stimulus, the baby can react in two different ways, (react or not)?

The obvious answer then must be, that the baby does NOT simply react to the outside stimulus, it is reacting to something else.

And just what might that something be? The only other type of information available to it, the mother.

To again return to our model, the baby learns through the parts of the mother's soul that she invests in it, but how does this explain the putting into place of the complex interactions of body, emotions and hormones?

The answer lies in the admitting of a new paradigm, that:

What we term as emotion is an ensemble of; body, emotions and hormonal reactions, which are intrinsically interconnected, in such a way, that, no matter which of the three is activated, it will, in turn activate the other two. It is, in short, no more and no less, than a 'package deal'.

Again the concept of particles, constructs and fields is useful, the construct 'emotion' is made up of three elements, each influencing the others.

So, where in story do the stimuli appear? In this model, the stimuli come later.

First, the three principle actors enter onto the scene, they learn how to interact with each other, and only then, after the triple link is in place, does the question of stimulus come into play.

This idea is attractive as it does away with the question of which reaction comes first, since any one is capable to incite the other two, but is there any research that could lend credence to this view?

7.3   The genesis of emotions:

In a study, carried out at Nagasaki University in Japan, ten pregnant volunteers were asked to watch an upbeat five-minute clip from the Julie Andrews musical, The Sound of Music.

Another 14 watched a tear-jerking five minutes from the 1979 Franco Zeffirelli film The Champ, in which a boy cries at the death of his father.

All the participants were wearing headphones, so it was impossible for the babies to hear anything from the films, hence they were blocked from any direct stimulus effect.

The researchers found that the foetuses moved their arms significantly more during the happy clip from The Sound of Music.

But in the other group, the unborn babies moved significantly less than normal while their mothers watched the weepie.

So what creates in the babies these reactions?

The mothers, while watching the positive movie, will have created within themselves the triple reaction; their dopamine levels will have increased, creating an experience of feeling good, which in turn, will have slowed the heart and generally relaxed the body.

(There is no guarantee as to the order of these reactions, in fact, I suggest that they all mutually stimulate and re-enforce each other).

What is important to note, is that the unborn baby is sensitive to all three manifestations within the mother.

The physical tension or relaxation of the mother's body has a direct effect on the baby; the flow of blood can be easily restricted if she is tense, as is the free movement within the uterus.

The Faculty of Medicine, Imperial College London, in a recent study have discovered that; that there is a highly significant correlation between maternal and foetal cortisol levels.

Which can only mean to say that either the baby already produces its own cortisol, (rather unlikely), or that these hormones are capable to pass from the mother's body, through the umbilical cord and into the baby.

The proof that the third piece of the jigsaw is possible, is that the baby is capable to capture and integrate the mother's emotional state.

One only needs to refer to our model, it is exactly this, that the baby integrates the mother's mental and emotions states through her sharing of those elements of her own soul.

Hence, it is possible to hypothesis that the growing foetus is capable to perceive all three of the mother's reactions to any given stimulus, **in absence of any part of the stimulus directly reaching it.**

Because it quickly learns that all three elements always appear together, (if not instantaneously, then in close proximity), it then proceeds to mimic this phenomenon and to also create the three as a linked group.

What this in fact means, is that, as soon as it receives a message that mother has produced one of the three elements, then it will notice that she will soon also produce the other two.

Hence, as soon as it experiences any one, it too will complete with the other two.

It is only later, when it has had the opportunity to experience various stimuli and to link them to different internal reactions that the emotional stimulus – response model comes into effect.

7.4   Any one of three?

This new model postulates that any one of the three reactions, body, emotional or hormonal, will act as a generator of the other two, but can that idea be defended?

We have already come across the model of cognitive stimulus – emotional response, which is now readily accepted as a trigger for hormonal and physical reactions.

Also, the tachycardia crisis has been shown to trigger anguish, fear or panic, with the resulting hormonal secretions quickly following suite.

But is there similar proof that a change in the hormonal balance also results in physical and emotional changes?

Well, the pharmaceutical companies would certainly have us believe in this supposition!

Certain anti-depressors are sold with the joint aim of not only improving mood, but also reducing the associated pains and aches that often accompany depression.

As generally, none-specific pains are often the result of holding the body in a state of tension; the thinking behind these products is that they will also have an effect of the somatic level.

By improving the mood through hormone manipulation, this will reduce the muscular tension, hence the pain will subside. (This is, of course a rather simplified description).

7.5.   Everybody is right!

So, to summarise, everybody is right.

Any of the three triggers will activate the process and set into motion the stimulation of the other two.

It only needs to be clarified that the cognitive stimulus – emotional response can be stimulated either from an outside stimulus that links directly to a particular memory / group of memories related to that object or subject, or it can indirectly awaken a memory, freely associated with the presented stimulus.

However, this response is perfectly capable to be activated by a train of thought that has no direct outside stimulus in the moment.

All that is important to keep in mind is that emotions are a package deal, whatever is the initial generator, all three levels will soon be activated.

By the same rule, the deactivation of the emotion can also be invoked through any one of the same three channels.

Food and drink can affect the production of certain hormones, talking to someone often helps us feel better and breathing exercises, sport and dance can act directly on the body.

We know, through experience, that any of the above, can create a positive effect.

The classic image of a young woman, sharing a large tub of ice-cream with her flat-mate after an emotional breakup is known to most.

As is the one of the male partner; drowning his sorrows in the local bar, baring his soul to his best friend, or the friendly barman.

The reduction of the strong, negative, emotive experience in any of the three dimensions, will also help the others to return to their normal level of functioning.

8. Early Stages

8.1 Birth, the 1st Separation & Meetings

So what changes during and after the moment of birth?

The physical separation of the baby and the mother is obvious, but what happens to the shared energy fields?

Keeping in mind the two, linked yet independent functions of psyche and soul, one first needs to reflect on the 'space' or the envelope that contains these functions.

Let us not forget that the energy surrounding the physical body space is only one manifestation of a 'psychic energy field', although it is the one that encompasses all the internal fields.

It is this particular field which delimits our personal space from those of all the others, however; it does NOT have the function of stopping our other energy fields from expanding outwards nor blocking the energy fields of others from entering into our individual space.

The psychic envelope, although separated from the mother's during or very soon after the birth, is still largely 'inhabited' by an important portion of her soul energy.

However this is only transitorily and if not re-enforced regularly, as with physical food and liquid, the little soul will start to 'starve'

Fortunately, very quickly after the birth, other people can also nourish the baby, even the presence of animals has been known to be sufficient.

I find that the simplest image to use is that one which follows the 'traditional' vision; which is to say, that part of the soul material of the mother, (or other), is projected into the baby.

This soul, energy stuff, is then used to nourish the baby and help it reinforce its own soul development.

Of course, if the baby is left alone for a few hours, from time to time, and even if it wakes up and starts to cry, but doesn't get any positive response, it won't die.

However, if this happens too often and for too long, there will be a heavy price to pay

At the same time it is important to reflect on, to imagine that she / they then begin to co-create a new energy field with the baby, in which is introduced a portion of their own psyche and soul material.

One could name that as their 'relationship field'.

8.2 The relationship field and transitional objects

8.3   The relationship field

The relationship field is a very important construct for the well-being of almost all human beings.

It can be understood as a form of ethereal body that is usually co-created between people and all living things.

However, it is possible to create a type of pseudo relationship field where only one of the persons invests energy, the input of the other is merely a fantasised projection.

This can create an unhealthy eroticised relation. I will return to this topic in the third volume when dealing with pathological relationship issues.

Every contact creates some form of relationship field, every shared experience, direct or indirect feeds that field and adds content.

It is this field that we activate when we think of someone, which, **depending of the active constructs of the moment** bring us joy, solace, security, disappointment anger, fear, etc.

It is a field that operates in the absence of the other, as it is created by ourselves and is 'ours'. (Which is to say that the other person also has their own version of that relationship field.)

As this field is 'ours' we can energise and invest it, 'at will', and the quantity of energy that we imbibe it with, at any moment is generally our own choice.

When we energise it, our soul stuff that exists within it, becomes activated and, as reflected above, brings us various sensations and emotions.

In fact, it is mainly the energising of these 'external' fields that generate sensations and emotions, but more of that later.

Relationship fields can also be linked to objects and other fields, posts, presents and pets fall into this category.

What then leads us on to the topic of transitional objects.

9. Transitional Objects – Myths and Realities

9.1 What we think we know:

The concept of a transitional object is well known, and seems to be well understood.

According to Wikipedia: 'A comfort object, transitional object, or security blanket is an item used to provide psychological comfort, especially in unusual or unique situations, or at bedtime for small children.'

In human childhood development, the term transitional object is normally used. It is something, usually a physical object, which takes the place of the mother-child bond.

Donald Woods Winnicott introduced the concepts of transitional objects and transitional experience in reference to a particular developmental sequence.

With "transition" Winnicott means an intermediate developmental phase between the psychic and external reality. In this "transitional space" we can find the "transitional object."

When the young child begins to separate the "me" from the "not-me" and evolves from complete dependence to a stage of relative independence, it uses transitional objects. Infants see themselves and the mother as a whole.

However, unless this process is severely faulty, it fails to explain why, according to a 2011 survey by Travelodge, about 35 percent of British adults still sleep with a teddy bear.

And, emergency vehicles and police patrol cars are sometimes equipped with stuffed toys, to be given to victims involved in an accident or traumatic shock and provide them comfort.

After the September 11 attacks, writes Marita Sturken in Tourists of History, "the Oklahoma City National Memorial sent six hundred teddy bears and then the state of Oklahoma sent sixty thousand stuffed animals to New York.

These were then distributed to children in schools affected by 9/11, family support organizations, and New York fire stations."

In my own practice I have met forty year old women, who, in moments of deepest crisis have resorted to searching for their 'tammy' to help calm them down.

The classic first scene in the film The Producers, where Leo Bloom,(Gene Wilder), has his blue blanket taken from him, creating obvious emotional distress, is not as ridiculous as all that.

9.2 A Mother substitute or What?

The soul body, like any other needs to be continually fed, so not to starve.

Relationship fields, because they hold a quantity of the soul energy of the other, nourish us when we activate them.

Because a baby is not yet aware of the existence of 'the other', it is not yet capable to construct relationship fields.

Hence, when left alone, (even in the physical presence of other people that are not giving it energy), it has nothing to 'feed itself' from.

In the non-contested theory of child development, the transitional object replaces the mother, which hitherto was experienced as a continuation of the child.

Who is now, more and more, becoming separated, leaving an anxiety provoking lack for the young child.

Referring back to our own model, this fits nicely to image of a continuing separation between the mother and the child, as she releases more and more of her energy from the child, so as to be able to focus on other life projects; (career, caring, creating, cleaning, cooking, etc…).

This distance taking, is a continuous process, beginning at the moment of birth, being the first instance of physical distance, which could be imagined as an experience of soul loss.

With the return of the mother, her, holding the child, being the first experiences of soul retrieval.

Of course the baby soon learns to invest in other people and animals into whose energy fields the child can enter and find safety, security and nourishment.

However, they too also leave, creating again this unpleasant experience of soul loss.

So, how can this little soul deal with repeating, painful experience? It takes its experiences of being loved and cared for and recreates within itself the elements necessary to sooth itself.

It learns to love and sooth itself through joining into a mutual space with the caregiver, (a more general and more realistic term, in many circumstances than 'mother').

By holding the child, just as the complex interaction of stimulus, hormonal, physical and emotion actions and reactions were learnt in the womb, now, various forms of discomfort and appropriate comforting actions become linked.

To this end, the repeated experience of soul loss becomes more and more copeable as the child learns to activate some form of replacement for itself.

Where the classic view and our model differ is in that, this is not a necessarily a transitional object, in as much as being a replacement object for the 'mother', but an externalisation of the carer and protector in ourselves.

It constructs a basic form of relationship field in which it uses an object as a physical support, **into which it invests its own soul energy.**

Remember, it cannot yet clearly distinguish between its own self and that of the other, so it is capable, to a limited degree to feed itself off from this.

As such, the object, (which often is no more than one's own thumb), becomes more and more invested with this function and, energetically, can take on a form, that is so linked to this experience, that just its presence can have a soothing and calming effect.

That it is an extension of the child, than a replacement for the 'mother', is, to some degree, quite easily proven.

In almost all cases, the object, (most often), a soft toy or blanket, must not be washed. The smell that is impregnated into it, is not that of the mother, but of the child itself.

It is however, reasonable and normal to wash the baby's thumb from time to time …

Hence, the 'transitional object' is not to replace the mother, rather, the experience of soul loss from its own envelope, by creating a substitute soul element.

This objet is partly within the intimate field of the baby, and yet outside of the physical envelope, it is thanks to that, that it can serve this function.

Of course, one could argue that in fact there is very little difference, and that this reflection is rather pointless, a point that certainly holds merit.

However, the idea that we can invest in things, even inanimate objects, that are, at least, capable to reflect back, positive, (and negative), energies, is an important reflection to have, as we look at how we can invest parts of our souls in pets, people and projects.

10. The Growth Process of the Psychic Envelope:

10.1   Food for thought

If one might image that the first representation of the soul, as a small, mostly white, malleable, spherical object, co-created and inherited from the mother, then we needs ask, how is it nourished and how does it grow?

As just stated, it is nourished mostly by human contact.

The simplest and most obvious image is the baby sucking on its mother's breast.

On the most basic, physical level, it is absorbing milk, physical nutriments, which helps its body to grow and to flourish.

However, many studies have shown that babies that have been breast fed for quite a long time succeed much better intellectually and socially in life than those that didn't.

The concept that the psyche develops through this contact is not at all new and was an important element in certain works by Melanie Klein.

One can easily imagine that in parallel with imbibing milk, the baby is also taking in another type of energy, an energy that is feeding its soul and as its soul increases in size, this allows more and more room for the cognitive functions to be put into place.

Of course it is not only through breast feeding mothers that babies succeed to get this form of nourishment and hence 'growth'.

All and any positive interaction allows the baby to suck energy from the person and hence to healthfully grow.

I stress here, 'positive' interaction as many babies and children suffer from abuse and or abandon in their early years, often due to the emotional lacks already experienced by their own parents.

These persons, if they do not succeed to find compensatory experiences later on in life, often end with quite debilitating psychological and emotional problems, although intellectual and socio- economic complications often also accompany these difficulties.

… More on this topic can be found in volume 3.

 So the baby connects to humans, animals and relatively quickly to transitional objects.

As long as the baby gets regularly stimulated and alimented from the outside, it will continue to grow and to thrive.

However, even a transitional object can take the place of a living being in case of total need.

Experiments in the 50's by Harry Harlow, showed that baby monkeys could 'invest' in a ragdoll as a mother figure. This ragdoll mother was sufficient to create a feeling of safety even when the baby was presented with a scary object, stimulus.

Also, in many studies, it has been shown that even very limited human contact, from a neutral care giver, (a nurse in an orphanage), held for a short time, but on a regular basis, can have a very important positive effect, compared to babies that lack even that minimum 'holding'.

As mentioned above, the cognitive functions; recognising a particular human voice or even the proximity of a person's presence, for instance, the difference between one person or another touching the mother's belly, start very early in the embryonic stage.

However, the quantity and intensity of information that passes into the womb is particularly limited when compared with the emergence into the real world.

What has already been put into place is the ability to perceive, to integrate and to remember.

Certain repeated stimuli have been shown to elicit the same responses and REM sleep, (a likely indication of mental integration) is experienced from the 7th month.

Newborn babies spend approximately 16 hours a day sleeping, half of this in REM sleep, this is likely to point to an enormous amount of processing of information, as all of the five senses are refining themselves and the system is simultaneously creating the ways and means to process and is processing this new information that is pouring in.

To a greater or lesser degree, this process is automatic and autonomous of human interaction; the biological blueprint, the hardwired coding, as long as the system has the minimum resources to function, it will continue to absorb and to integrate all the information in its immediate surroundings, create schemas and patterns of them and continue to build its own capacities to survive.

It is at this level that we can understand the value of Rupert Sheldrake's work on morphogenetic fields.

For instance, locomotive skills, movement and coordination, are something that will happen, sooner or later, through trial and error, without any necessary intervention from another person.

However, a minimum level of physical and emotional support and nourishment is necessary even for these 'natural' processes to occur.

There is a syndrome, (Failure to thrive), that can block both physical and cognitive progress, if these two dimensions are not sufficiently catered for.

On the UK netsite, www.patient.co.uk *, we find, amongst the 'Non-organic or 'functional' causes of FTT':

Lack of preparation for parenting.

Family dysfunction (eg, divorce, spouse abuse, chaotic family style).

A difficult child.

Child neglect (there may be puerperal depression).

Emotional deprivation syndrome.

However, where human interaction is critical is when the baby needs to understand the sense of information; be it physical, emotional or cognitive.

*. http://www.patient.co.uk/doctor/growth-and-failure-to-thrive

10.2 The first learning experiences interoception

(An internal sense also known as interoception is "any sense that is normally stimulated from within the body")

In the very early stages of life; the baby will experience moments of discomfort when it might or might not know what it needs; tiredness, hunger, also physical discomfort due to needing changing or turning or colic.

Sometimes it has reflexes that help us show where the problem lies; (a baby can smell a women who is lactating and will turn its head in her direction and make sucking movements, when hungry).

Through sensitivity; good sense and often a process of trial and error, the carer will find the cause of the problem and alleviate the suffering.

This process, which continues on through the whole of childhood, and in some cases, (in the sense of a psychotherapy, personal and spiritual work), through into later life, helps the baby, child, person to learn to read their own signals of discomfort and find a solution.

By the simple act of responding appropriately to the baby's needs, it begins to differentiate the different internal signals until it becomes aware of from where the discomfort originates.

(For a number of reasons, even some adults refuse or ignore their own inner signals, this is more than unlikely to be due to a lack of childhood integration.)

Likewise; any stimulus that is strong, (load noises, flashing lights, physical sensations etc...,) will give the baby cause for alarm and for a certain distress.

However, learning how to respond from outside, exteroceptive signals is slightly different.

10.3   The first learning experiences exteroception

One of the first systems of understanding the world and its signals is through (social) referencing.

The baby experiences something, it then looks to another being, it seeks out the reaction of that other to create a stimulus – response reaction of its own.

To begin with, its reaction is likely to be experienced and expressed in the moment, only to be forgotten straight after.

If the reaction of the other is strong enough or repeated often, then this becomes integrated in the baby's psyche.

We have already seen this referencing, learning process at work during the embryonic stage when the baby notices a stimulus, (the sound of a voice, a physical contact).

The mother responds in a positive manner, (pleasure hormones, muscle relaxation), and the baby learns that this is good and soon begins itself to react in the same way to the same input.

[Although, it must of course not be neglected, that a mother that is anxious, nervous or depressed during pregnancy, is likely to transmit these negative experiences to her unborn child.

The effect of psychological un-wellness during pregnancy, Werner *et al.* found that physiological markers of individual differences in infant temperament are identifiable in the fetal period, and possibly shaped by the prenatal environment. Antenatal psychiatric diagnosis was also associated with a fourfold increase in cry reactivity in infants.]

Referencing, later developed into a clear system of social referencing is a fundamental way that the baby learns how to react and respond to our complex world.

So, what happens to the developing psyche in these instances?

The awareness of a stimulus enters into the psychic space.

The 'question' of how to respond is activated.

As long as there is no particular answer to this question, there is discomfort.

If the stimulus is strong, intense or cannot be avoided, removed or ignored this is likely to create an experience called pain.

This pain takes energy out of the soul of the baby.

When a care giver appears, the baby looks to that person to answer its question and to alleviate its suffering.

This person is there to sooth the infant, (whether or not they themselves are tired, irritated or what-ever), and the child feels already the benefit or not having to face this problem alone.

The attention of the person returns some energy to the soul of the baby.

At the same time, often through the care givers' monologues, (many mothers and nurses talk all the time to 'their' babies, although men tend to be less verbose), the baby is calmed and explained to.

This communication enters into the psychic space, (or relationship field), and starts to create a response to the 'question'.

This response, is contextual, every detail of the situation has some value in its creation.

Even though, especially during the early years, most, if not all these details will be lost, something of that event becomes imprinted.

Through repeated events, certain of the details become more and permanent, most often linked to the person or persons involved.

In fact, through this interaction, a tiny portion of the soul of the other is projected into the child.

In situations of trauma, the details become engraved into the psyche and their ability to link to the dramatic event becomes a major problem, but more of that later on.

These 'responses' become more and more permanent and each one can be imagined as a type of psychic building 'block'.

As mentioned, since these experiences are contextual and include many different dimensions; the blocks themselves are multi-dimensional, hence multi-faceted.

From the perspective of field dynamics, the event itself can be seen as a form of energy.

This energy then creates a particle, which, being unknown and strange, causes discomfort in the system, as the young child doesn't know how to deal with it, and where and with what to put it.

The care giver, in parallel with their expressed behaviour and emotions, also activates a micro field, in which this particle is linked to certain psychic blocks. This field and the construct within it, expresses their own history and reaction to the event.

The care giver envelops that child in a protective field, in which that micro-field exists. The child then uses this model to link the particle to one or several blocks of its own.

Hence a micro field is then created, joining the first event particle with the psychic block(s), in which a reaction is generated, eventually forming a relatively stable miniature subsystem.

In short the other, (adult or even child), has succeeded to pass on information on how to experience this phenomenon.

Over time, the psyche links enough similar events and responses to create a general field, which is then capable to deal, not only with known phenomena, but with unexperienced yet similar events.

From that point onwards, every time that an event of that nature occurs, that field is activated, the linked response is read and actioned and the event is integrated into the field as a re-enforcement of the field dynamic.]

By bringing together a number of these experiences, patterns have begun to emerge.

These images can also be likened to a punched card, which held a small bit of programming for early computers.

The baby finds itself in a situation which is causing it some discomfort or distress, it looks through its blocks to find those that have some elements linked to the situation.

It separates them from the rest and sees how it might put them together to create a working pattern which will respond to the 'question', which-is-to-say, how to stop the discomfort.

The child then 'runs that pattern', (Nb nothing to do with American football, I think), or that little bit of program, to continue to use that image.

The situation could be something like this; 'no one is giving me any attention, I feel bad, (my soul is shrinking),

I drop teddy, I cry, mommy picks it up, she smiles at me, she gives me attention, I feel better, (my soul is nourished)'.

However, it is likely that the same game will not work with everyone and the child quickly learns that if she tries that with her brother, he will not give it back to her but hide it under a chair!

Hence the program begins to complexify and two subroutines are formed:

1. Stimulus ; I am being ignored, I have an object, there is someone here, not my brother.
Response: I drop the object.

2. Stimulus ; I am being ignored, I have an object, there is someone here, it is my brother.
Response: I do not drop the object.

It is here that our model and Sheldrake's basic morphogenetic model part company.

The patterns that are created are constantly open to change and evolution. They work on all the data available in the moment, including the physical, emotional, and mental states of all the important protagonists at this precise moment.

Hence, the person is capable to react differently in many situations, even if they might seem identical when seen from the outside.

This ability create, re-create, modify and release constructions is what makes all living things capable to survive and flourish.

The more adaptable a species might be, then the more capable that species is to survive. Many woodland and forest creatures have now adapted to live in cities. Those that have not succeeded to make the transition are in danger of extinction.

The human being has become more and more the master of adapting.

11. Next Steps

11.1 First Constructs

The psychic envelope including the soul dimension continues to grow and to be nourished by those people, animals and things that surround the child. Animals and objects can play an important role in its emotional development and experiences of being loved, feeling safe and being protected.

And those close to him continue to share their understanding of his / her experiences so that the child succeeds to integrate its actions, reactions and feelings into an identifiable psychological composition.

For its part, the child has learnt to give and receive energy, and even if it still uses the energy of others, so as to maintain its own growth momentum, it now also creates its own energy both for itself and to share with others.

It should here be noted, that most, if not all of us, on some level or other need other people to exchange energy with, to keep our souls, 'full and healthy'.

Not forgetting that our relationships with children and animals might well bring us much more, and better quality energy than we might get from many of our human, adult compatriots!

One needs to keep in mind that the child, (as with all sentient beings), captures every sight, sound and sensation that it presented with. Every sigh, every shrug, every shift of attention, is registered and processed.

Self-awareness, on almost all levels is NOT hard wired into the system; it has to be slowly, patiently and sometimes, even painfully, learnt.

Just watch a baby working on learning how to coordinate its hand, how to make it move, to stop, to grasp, to bring and then to release.

It is almost the same process when a child is tired; it might well experience, irritability, confusion, impatience but young children often do not know when they are feeling tired.

Sources of emotional pain are also often very difficult for the child to differentiate; 'why do you think that you are feeling; angry, sad, jealous …?'

Of course, even as adults we still have moments when we are not conscious of our reactions or the sources of these reactions, but that is more likely to be due to an unconscious choice to dis-acknowledge the reaction /source, based on certain value judgements and self-image issues.

11.2 Explicit Messages

At the most basic level, one might say that the young child is in some sort of constant survival quest. As it certainly cannot survive alone, it must react appropriately to continue to receive the nourishment that it needs to continue to live and to thrive.

Watching a two year old throwing a tantrum because he cannot have the sweets he wants you to buy him at the supermarket checkout, does not intuitively support this view. However, I suggest that somewhere, on some level, he feels safe enough to express this 'bad' behaviour.

Take a (very) hypothetical situation, the child starts to ask for the sweets; the parent says no, the child insists, the parent warns the child that if he doesn't stop asking for the sweets immediately he will be physically punished, now, here in the shop.

The child persists but only, at this stage, to demand.

The parent, with or without showing emotion, physically and quite severely chastises the child.

The child will not have to experience this situation many times before it stops asking for sweets at the checkout.

In this particular case it would be the physical pain that would be the punishment that changes or creates a behaviour modification, but in everyday life there are other, much more subtle messages and punishments; the sigh, the shrug, and the shift of attention, (as well of course of the contrary, re-enforcing behaviour reactions).

Why is it the sigh, the shrug, and the shift of attention, which I have listed, over and above that of the spoken word?

11.3 Implicit Messages

Long before the child begins to understand, let alone control language, it is already acutely aware of its surroundings and the positive and negative reactions of people to each other and to itself. That awareness is surely, almost totally unconscious, but it is assuredly there.

Not only are these messages picked up very early in the child's life but, being non-verbal, and therefore, for the most part below the level of conscious awareness, they continue to have a very strong, re-enforcing effect, all throughout its life.

We all learn through experience; whether, for the most part, through the direct help and overt reactions of other people as suggested by writers like the Russian, Lev Vygotsky, or mostly alone and independently, as suggested by Piaget in his work in Geneva.

We are also to quite a large degree, programmed through positive and negative feedback: as proposed by the Americans, John B. Watson and B. F. Skinner.

However, new concepts such as dynamic systems theory, (Esther Thelen, from the USA), and social referencing (Elizabeth Fivaz in Lausanne), are now much more in vogue.

What they all have in common is that as (new) information enters into the system, it is processed by a validating procedure that compares it to both intellectual and emotional data in the past and in the present.

That might sound a little complicated. Let's take a real life example to see what this means and how it functions.

The child is sitting, inactive, it looks to a caregiver, (silently asking for attention), the caregiver either responds and proposes an activity, (Vygotsky) or ignores the child and continues what they are doing, (Piaget).

The child (re)acts, the adult then responds in some way to the child's endeavours, giving positive or negative feedback, (Behaviourism, DST, Social referencing).

In the first case, the child is given attention, it smiles at the caregiver, who smiles back. Hence, looking for attention becomes a positive and useful strategy.

In the second scenario, the child is ignored. It can then either increase its demand for attention by crying or throwing something, or not bother, and give up trying.

In the case of increased demand, the care giver can either give the child the attention that it craves, which quietens down the exchange and everyone is okay. Only the child has its first message that to get attention, one needs to 'make a noise'.

However, if it is still ignored, then it will eventually realise that it won't get any attention and will occupy itself and either become more and more independent or, quite the opposite, it will become timid and introverted.

If, on the other hand, the child is punished for this behaviour it might learn that it is only by excessive demands that it can get attention and it learns that being 'bad' has some benefits, or it becomes anxious and nervous.

If the child does not get enough positive feedback, then they might quickly integrate that it is not worth looking for attention, as it won't get it. In this case, it either becomes another Piaget or a very timid introvert, living more and more in its own, protected world.

This way the reaction is then added to and compared to past experiences and then the behaviour is re-enforced or not or even suppressed.

One very important reflection on behaviour, (attitudes, beliefs, desires etc.,) that have been suppressed, is that this does not at all mean that these elements no longer exist within the child, only that they no longer have the possibility to express themselves at this time, in this environment.

At what point in their lives they might wish to, need to and / or succeed to express them again, only time and circumstances can only tell.

This topic will be further discussed in the chapter on the conscious and the unconscious.

11.4 On the nourishing of the soul and the psychic envelope:

The child becomes more and more an actor in the maintenance of its soul. It has learned how to increase its own well-being by amusing, caring and looking after itself.

It intentionally generates soul energy which it gives out to those in its environment, having learned through positive re-enforcement that this will increase its own happiness.

However, as with any form of nourishment, if he cannot get 'food' that brings pleasure and leaves a 'nice taste in the mouth', then he will take whatever he can, and settle for that.

As mentioned above, there exists a diagnosis of 'Failure to Thrive', where the young child does not grow or gain weight as it should.

(There is also a similar problem in old age).

Johns Hopkins children's centre, on its net site:
http://www.hopkinschildrens.org/Failure-to-Thrive.aspx.

Lists one of the external causes of this problem as
Emotional Deprivation, which is now recognised as a
clinical disorder in its own right.

Also, if you are interested in the subject, you might
find the following piece interesting.

Baars, Conrad W. & Anna A. Terruwe. Healing the
Unaffirmed: Recognizing Emotional Deprivation
Disorder. Rev. ed. Suzanne M. Baars and Bonnie N.
Shayne (eds.) Staten Island, NY: ST PAULS/Alba
House, 2002

Hence the young child needs, in any way possible to
avoid emotional deprivation, even if it results in
continual negative feedback.

Unfortunately, negative feedback itself can create
further future problems, but as the immediate need is to
grow and survive, that is where the priority lies.

12 On the building of the psychic machine:

12.1 Informational elements:

As stated before, everything that the child experiences enters into his psychic envelope.

At the first level there are experiences and information that have no emotional or relationship content, but go into its knowledge base and add to its basic technical competences, (physical, intellectual and mechanical evolution), learning to move, refining of all 5 senses, simple recognition of people and objects, etc...

These informations and attributes quickly become integrated into the basic functioning of the system and unless or until they dis-function in some ways, they cease to affect us consciously. In themselves they have no emotional, no soul energy or content.

Everything else that enters into the system has some possible energy content.

There are masses of general information that also have no direct or obvious emotional or relationship value on their own.

12.2   Neutral Elements

However, any piece of information might be or become linked to an emotional event; the smells of ritual foods on high holidays, the flowers from a wedding or a funeral, the colour of a wall in the maternity ward.

For the most part, these informations if not often repeated are temporarily stocked and quickly forgotten.

What needs to be clear is that all psychic blocks are a fusion of information and energy. They have a psychic, cognitive dimension, yet they are also created of soul material, which might also be expressed as emotions.

Which means that can change shape, form and colour, (to give some imagery here), their size and hence the importance to the person is immensely variable.

One should note that the intensity of the emotional experience during their moment of creation has a major influence on their future place and importance in the psychic space.

In general, most daily experiences can be likened to balloons, they enter into the psychic space of a certain size, they float around for a moment, easy to see and to notice.

Quite quickly the air starts to escape; they deflate and eventually are collected up and stocked in some cupboard or other, on the off chance that they might be of some future interest or use.

After some further while, there is a deeper tidying up made, they are now totally deflated and they are then tightly boxed up in crates of similar experiences, which become a type of compacted, consolidated, memory unit.

These memory units still retain the emotional shape and colour that they originally possessed.

Over time, these memory units might even be associated with other memory units and further consolidated, but, although some deterioration might well occur, especially with time, most of the experiences can still be accessed if it becomes important to reconnect to them.

In short, the balloon can be re-inflated at any time, which is to say that they can be re-infused with (soul) energy and then linked to other related experiences.

However, for any number of reasons, one or many of today's balloons attracts my attention, that attention reflates the balloon and keeps it floating somewhere in my consciousness.

Every time I give it attention, I infuse it with energy, with soul, then it grows and retains its place. Obviously the bigger it gets, the longer it will subsequently take to deflate and disappear into the recesses of my psychic space.

Also by linking various elements together, each re-enforces the presence of the other, which works as part of our cognitive, learning processes.

If for some reason they then are linked to a psychic block, then this energy source can keep them activated indefinitely.

12.3 Charged Elements

We now come to a much more complex process; units that are charged with a strong emotional energy. The first important differentiation to make, is from where comes the charge.

When the charge comes from outside ourselves, the unit carries within it, energy, soul material from the people or thing that were involved in the experience.

Clearly, the intensity of the experience and their reaction is of a certain value, however, your relationship with them, directly or indirectly can be of much more importance.

In the initial creation of the importance of that block, must be taken into consideration, the number and size of other blocks that you already have which link to this one. (We might use the concept of block size to express the amount of energy that it carries).

When the charge comes from inside ourselves, this is, if anything, much more complicated. We are, as is being discussed, to some degree, only a sum of all our experiences.

If we are having a strong reaction to an event, it must be in part due to other events in our past that we resonate with or to.

Hence, this event must link to other events, which themselves, must already carry quite an emotional charge, which is to say, carry a lot quantity of soul material.

From the field theory point-of-view, similar experiences or psychic blocks, interact to create their own particular fields. The more energy that each block carries and more blocks that are assembled within the field, increases the fields' potential. The stronger the field, the more easily it attracts other, less similar experiences or sub-fields into its field of influence and the effect that it has on the person.

However, one must not forget, that even if a field that is constituted within the unconscious meta-field, becomes particularly powerful, that in no way means that it will necessarily become conscious.

What it does mean, is that, on some level, it will greatly influence the person, hidden in the unconscious region, in ways beyond the awareness of that person.

This explains much in the realms of unusual or unreasonable attitudes or behaviours, and is, not surprisingly, often the root of psychological distress.

Before going on any further with these reflections, we must stop for a moment and reflect on the Conscious, Unconscious and the Forgotten.

13. The Conscious the Unconscious and the Forgotten

13.1 Basic concepts

Before reflecting on the creation, feeding and processing of these fields, we will need to understand what we mean by these terms.

The conscious is the space where we have access to knowledge, thoughts and feelings.

The unconscious also houses knowledge, thoughts and feeling, yet we have no direct awareness of their existence, hence, no control of accessing them, other than asking ourselves if something 'feels' right or not

This also works on the level of intuition, which is discussed elsewhere within this work.

There is also, within the model, an intermediate area, this is where 'forgotten' experiences are stocked. These are the psychic blocks that hold little energy in themselves and hence drift out of the conscious meta field towards the unconscious.

We use the term 'meta-field' here, as all the knowledge, experiences and sensations that we have ever experienced, exist in one of these three fields.

However, a psychic block, being a complex but simple unit, can still be included in any number of individual fields, which can transverse all three meta fields.

Which is to say, any field can include; conscious, forgotten and unconscious constructs. This explains how a conscious thought can also activate 'stuff' that has been forgotten and, in parallel, unconscious experiences.

So how comes that some groups of blocks live in the conscious areas of our psychic space and others in the unconscious part?

Actually, from a topographical point of view, there is no separation between conscious and unconscious; there is not a 'place' for each of the two groups. They contain the same elements linked to their creation; the cognitive informations, the links to other blocks and the soul contents from those involved in their making and the emotional / soul links to all other related blocks.

Many blocks contain information that is marked by the energy / person / situation from which it came. Which is to say; we can often remember and define from where, when and whom a certain action, remark or attitude came from.

Hence blocks generated by parental figures tend to be the most present during early life.

However, it also very often happens that certain blocks are created without our conscious awareness or interest of from where the information has been generated.

This is very often the case of blocks that come from sources of very little interest to us; we overhear a stranger mentioning that it is likely to rain tomorrow; we read in a paper on a park bench, that the economy is in trouble, we smell the smoke of a neighbour having a barbeque.

What the fundamental difference between these two is; is that the elements of the first group find an affinity in one or more fields within the meta-conscious field, but not from the second, which slip 'silently' directly into the unconscious field.

However, if we 'notice' a piece of information, which is to say that we are conscious of its existence, then it becomes linked to certain fields that then link it to other blocks within that field and then there other fields and so on.

On the other hand, there are the cases where we might or might not notice, (the importance of), a reaction or a behaviour; a smile, a sigh, a shrug, so we do not consciously link it to other factors in the environment.

As the reaction seems to have little informational value, and does not link to a conscious field it quickly melts into the forgotten.

However, the unconscious, which, not being distracted by trying to understand, deal with and react to everything that is happening in the moment, is able to capture the reaction and the whole context in which it is being expressed. – This case in point, we will return to below.

And, as we have also already seen, many, many of the small, unimportant daily events lose their specific energy and got stored away.

They lose the conscious connections to the fields on that meta-level, as their importance has been seen to be particularly limited. (The analogy of balloons)

How this happens is that; as the initial energy starts to drain out, it slips out of the conscious field, as if that field was a huge net and as the element 'shrinks', it falls through the hole into the 'forgotten', realm.

Another image that could be helpful is to imagine the three meta-fields on a vertical plane; the conscious region is at the top, in the sunlight, the forgotten part is lower down, bathed in shadow, while the unconscious is hidden in the depths of a dark pit.

To continue with the balloon analogy; the elements that are full of energy, float high in our consciousness's, if the energy seeps away, the balloon drops into the shadows, while the balloons that have 'heavy weights' attached to them, even if fully capable to link to conscious fields, will be 'condemned' to the hidden regions.

13.2.1 Reactions to explicit negative feedback

To understand what these 'heavy weights' might be, we need to return to a situation noted above, where the child had learned not to ask for attention because he would get none or negative feedback.

(An intentional lack of feedback, where the adult is aware of the demand, but chooses not to respond, can also be considered as a form of negative feedback).

Certain desires, attitudes and behaviours, etc., that are deemed unaccepted by the people / parents / care givers, which the child feels incapable to either defend or to release will end up in the unconscious field.

That which is considered as interesting, useful and acceptable is attracted into the conscious field, that which is not, is rejected by the conscious field, and hence is left to 'float' in the unconscious field.

However, the motivation to continue a particular type of behaviour can well be re-enforced by messages that escape our conscious awareness, and hence also live in the unconscious.

When we receive negative feedback, we are faced with four choices;

- A   to stop and change our behaviour, (way of functioning, beliefs etc…,),
- B   to rebel and continue, even in the face of opposition,
- C   thirdly, to stop the behaviour but rebel internally and consciously or finally;
- D   to stop the behaviour and to seem to accept that it is wrong, but, (unconsciously), to continue to believe that it is appropriate for us. It is in the last case in which we sublimate or repress our own reaction.

If we cannot accept any of the first three choices, we are only left with the possibility to hide our own rebellion from ourselves and to stock it in an inaccessible space, in short, the unconscious.

(To be deeply in conflict with those to whom our very lives depend, and / or who we love deeply, can be very psychologically painful; hence to repress is often the only solution.)

Although quite complex, this situation is fairly easy to visualise; the child's behaviour is a group of blocks that are held in their particular field. As is that of the authority figure.

These fields exist within a larger field, (family, school, society).

So now we have two fields; the child's behaviour, (cb), the negative reaction of the authority figure, (af), all enclosed within a greater field, the global context, (gc) of the conflict.

- A   The size or strength of field (af) is much more powerful than the child's (cb), so the child gives up.
  The child's field weakens and the blocks are reconfigured in a similar fashion to that of those in the authority' field.

- B   The desire of child is very important, the field (cb) is then powerful enough to withstand that of the of authority (af) and there is enough 'space' within the situation, context (gc), hence the two fields can co-exist and the child feels the possibility to rebel.

If the adults cede, then their field will be modified by the child's, if they don't give up then their field will continue to exist, but the possibility to rebel will have further re-enforced the child's field.

- C   The desire of child is very important, the field (cb) is then more important than that of authority (af) but there is not enough 'space' within the situation, context (gc), hence the child finds no possibility to rebel openly but continues to rebel internally.

-

One could imagine that the energy field of the child is englobed by that of the adults, but continues to exist.

- D   The desire of child is very important, but the field (af) is more powerful than his (cb) also there is no 'space' within the situation, context (gc), hence the child finds no possibility to rebel openly or internally.

-

The energy field of the authority figures fills all the space in the 'conscious' part of the context field.

However, as all fields can span all three regions of the psyche, there still exists space to forget or to repress / sublimate the energy.

Depending if the subject of the conflict is really important to the child or just a strong desire of the moment, will prove the ability for him just to forget the incident, (the balloon will un-swell and fall off into the forgotten realm or not.

If there is much 'charge' in the situation, and it is really important, for some reason to the child, it is unlikely that it will be forgotten, so the only place left is that of the unconscious.

It is this suppressed material which all too often become the source of much psychological and emotional suffering.

However, this is not the worst of the possible scenarios.

In this situation, the person can often remember the conflict, which can then be linked to the suppressed desire, and return it back to consciousness.

13.3 Reactions to implicit negative feedback

Remember; the sigh, the shrug, and the shift of attention? Yes, these also enter into the realm of negative feedback.

However, as mentioned, because they are often not consciously registered nor linked to a current 'event', the conscious mind takes little notice.

The child does not consciously realise that the parent, (ect.,) is sending out a message, however, on an energetic, soul level, he is informing the child that what it is doing, or saying, or experiencing or even being, is somewhere, somehow not acceptable.

Without this cognitive, open information, the child, although totally linking this negative feedback to the person, and situation, does not consciously register the information, no referencing, often no memory and no conscious trace, only another blank face, on another psychic block.

The same set of non- verbal, para-verbal or indirect information or messages, constitutes what in systemic therapy theory are called 'family secrets'.

This is where the child receives information linked to part of it's or the family's past without any clear, digital information. Only none specific emotional reactions, unlinked phrases, unsupported attitudes and demands of types of behaviour.

As there are no ways to link or index these experiences they too rest orphaned, hanging around the psychic space creating problems without solutions.

[Why do some of these unconscious blocks cause problems for the individual? That is one of the questions that we will save for the section of pathology and psychological un-wellness.]

It is not only particular behaviours that a child exhibits that can become repressed, what one very often sees in therapy is the repression of what I term, the 'true history'.

A child is presented with a 'reading' of certain of their own life events, which somewhere do not fit with a deep 'intuitive' feeling of another 'reality'.

This separation between the 'official history' and the 'true' but the inaccessible, unconscious version often leads to mental distress.

This subject will also be further developed in the therapeutic section in volume 3.

Another important reflection to have is that these subtle messages are almost always not conscious to the emitter. Which means to say, that the messages are coming from their unconscious.

Looking at the interaction from the aspect of energy fields; one could also imagine that some information passes directly from the unconscious field of the adult, into the unconscious field of the child.

]

13.4 Final Reflections on the Conscious the Unconscious and the Forgotten

In all three fields, conscious, unconscious and forgotten, there exists the possibility of limitless subfields, through which, these elements or particles can be activated and agglomerated to create; thoughts, memories, behaviours, reflexes and / or reactions.

These sub-groups affect us in many different ways, on all possible levels; physical, mental and emotional.

The unconscious field is nourished by two processes, repressed thoughts, feelings and emotions that are, on some level unacceptable, and those that enter directly because they have little emotional energy to keep them or link them with conscious elements.

We now see where the Freudian view of the unconscious, being the stocking depot of repressed desires, finds its place.

However, in our view, the unconscious does not only house negative repressed wishes and desires, the more generous vision of the American hypnotherapist Milton Erickson, of the unconscious stocking also many positive resources seems to be much more realistic

Why this should be so deserves to be reflected on.

Repressed thoughts, feelings and emotions do not have only to be negative. As we will see in the next chapter; who we are, who we express yourselves as and who other people see us as, are all different and changeable.

However, there are certain 'patterns' that become more or less fixed, and we are then incapable to express ourselves otherwise.

Any trait or expression that doesn't 'fit' into 'who we are', must then also be suppressed. That means if someone 'is'; a nice fool, a child, weak, timid, incompetent, mean etc., then any expression that does not fit into that image can not be accepted and so becomes hidden away.

But that is not all.

As we have seen, the unconscious also houses all information that we have been in contact with. These psychic blocks form and reform into an infinite combination of fields.

Even though we have no direct access to these fields, they exist and can be of enormous value.

In a group that I focalise, we work with a huge range of 'energies'; the four elements, all of nature, the animal kingdom, images of jobs and professions, as well as symbols like trains, hovercrafts etc.

Each and all of these energies exist within us. In this group, I work with the participants to contact with and to use these energies in the appropriate situations.

They can only do this because these energies, or psychic blocks ALREADY exist within them.

Hence, the unconscious also includes a vast storehouse of positive and useful resources, not to mention the 'intuitive' function, but that is also for further on in this work.

14. Who am I?

14.1 When do I become a who?

One's first reaction might well be, 'what an odd question', yet before one can imagine to answer, 'who am I?, we need to reflect on at what moment one becomes a 'person'.

Each of us is a unique creation, from my own experience as a father, I know that each being brings something into the world at the time of birth.

Whether that being has already been heavily conditioning while in the womb is of course impossible to answer, but in any case, arriving into our world, there is already 'someone there'.

Obviously, depending on your belief system, how much of the baby is in fact linked to an eternal soul, evolving soul, part of Universal matter, etc., is part of one's own life vision.

But it is clearly much too soon to talk of that little mass of feelings as a formed person.

Maybe we could choose the point when it starts to talk as the moment in question.

Many psychologists, philosophers, astrologers and mystics believe that there is a major change that occurs at seven years old.

Also, in many traditions, one becomes of age between 12 and 14 years old.

Although in the west the age of majority has moved from twenty one down to eighteen, in the world of astrology, the moment of maturity doesn't arrive until the first 'Saturn return', at approximately twenty-eight years old.

So, who is right?

Of course none and all are.

Each step and stage brings their own dimension of unity and completion.

However, one mustn't forget that one can and should continue to grow and change all our lives.

So, how do we answer this question?

First we need to look at what makes up the person.

From the point of view of our model, the identity of a person is made up of three constituents;

How others see them
How they express themselves as a person
How the person sees themselves

The order listed is of a certain importance.

14.2   How others see us:

What others project unto us; how they see us, what they expect of us, what they don't expect of us, can begin to be created even during the childhood of the parent.

Many children have roles and responsibilities imputed to them long before they are born.

One of the most current, (unfortunately), is the saviour of a couple, but that is far from the only one.

It is totally usual and normal to dream into an unborn child, in fact, as already stated, the dreaming into the child is part of its creation.

Hence, it needs be clear that this process of the creation of the identity of a person through these three constituents; is normal and necessary. It is only when this process is disturbed that it can become pathological.

As the process continues and other people 'participate' in the dream, the image grows and changes.

Surely this exercise never ceases, we can always change our image of someone based on feedback and information gleaned from others.

After the child's birth, this process continues, however, it complexifies even further, as the projections are now linked to the feedback from the child itself.

What is particularly interesting from the point of view of our model, and where it links in with Sheldrake's ideas, is that this image of the child, gives a certain 'blueprint' for the future 'shape' of the person's identity.

Returning to the concept of morphogenetics, the identity field is to a large degree created and re-enforced by the plan formed by those that bring us up.

In relation to our model, every person that has an image of us creates a unique field, in which we are 'expected' to fit. This expectation creates the same type of plan found in the work on morphogenetics, only it is merely a suggestion of a plan, not 'the' plan.

The more people, or the more these people are important, then the more influence these 'suggestions' can have.

However, we are certainly not only the product of our 'entourage'.

14.3   How we express ourselves as a person

The child arrives into this world with very clear personality traits.

For many years I was fairly convinced that the nature / nurture argument was overrated. I believed that it was mainly the environment that shaped the individual and the genetic / pre-birth component counted for little.

After assisting to the birth of my children, it became un-arguable and obvious that, even minutes after birth, the baby displays clear personality traits.

Throughout our lives; our basic, intrinsic personality traits will always be, to some degree or other expressed.

How much these deepest parts of who we are have the space to be expressed and re-enforced is unique to each of us.

Also, through our 'genetic plasticity', (not a concept accepted by all), and life experiences, within our possibilities, we are capable to find many, many different ways to be.

An aside note on 'genetic plasticity', (a concept that I have just coined). Just as every baby is born with the capacity to understand and speak any language from any part of the world. We have the potential within, (almost) all of us to express almost any characteristics, if and when it becomes necessary.

This is not an empty theoretical idea. We hear stories, regularly, of people that have gone well beyond or totally outside their usual behaviour or capacities in a survival situation.

This is also often the goal of personal therapy, or growth work.

However, to access and express these hidden parts of oneself, there is one major obstacle to overcome.

14.4   How we see ourselves

This is the meeting point between; how we express ourselves as a person and how others see us.

What is particularly important not to forget is that this is our reality. We see and believe ourselves to be 'who we are', with all the positive and negatives that this implies.

Because this is a truth, many of us become trapped in this reality, even if we are unsatisfied with our lives and ourselves.

From the point of view of our model, the way we see ourselves is a relatively fixed combination of energy blocks that form the foundation for the diverse forms that we express.

The idea that we express ourselves differently in any particular moment of our lives, will be discussed at some length a little further down.

14.5   The stages of being us

At birth; it is easy to project almost anything on a baby. It has no sense of self, and all its actions and reactions are at the basic program level.

At one year old; the baby has clearly separated as a unique person, it still lacks the apparatus for any intellectual self-awareness. While it's behaviour gives enough material for the entourage to begin to interpret its actions to fulfil certain of their expectations and desires.

By two years old the child is starting to realise that it can have an influence on the outside world, the famous period of 'no' or more generally known as the 'terrible two's'. This can be a difficult time for the outside images to hold, but people are really good at adapting outside realities to fit into their inner needs.

A parent that has experienced being abused as a child, will likely experience this first rebellious phase as something quite positive, and directly or indirectly support this expression.

By around three years old, the child has enough understanding to start to consciously integrate the parents and other adult's expressed wishes and desires.

However, it has already starting to integrate many other informations, from their behaviour, none-verbal and para-verbal actions and reactions.

Through these multiple inputs, the child has already started to adapt its behaviour and its vision of reality, both external and internal.

Throughout all these years all the 'bodies' that were mentioned before, are growing. These bodies can also be understood as specific types of fields.

One of the fields that creates the greatest protection against other people's fields is the mental (body), field. This creates an increasingly powerful filter.

According to many different views, as mentioned above, there is major change at seven years old. From my own personal and professional observations, the age range can range from five to nine years old, depending on the mental apparatus of the child.

From an outside point of view, the child's development becomes much more stable, the psycho-analysts term this as the latency period.

From our model's view point, the integration of the mental field has greatly reinforced the personal fields through which the child has been constantly been invaded by the energy from the outside.

From this quieter space, the child can more stabilise the field that can be termed as its identity field.

[A full reflection and discussion on this concept will be further dealt with at a later part of this work.]

At this point, there is usually a balance between the three influences; outside, inside and innate.

This more peaceful state of affairs usually holds until (pre) adolescence, when there is not only major physical and hormonal changes, but also many increasing social influences.

The effects of the physical and hormonal changes are in no way negligible, they create major changes in many of the energy (bodies), fields.

The most important for this reflection, is that the child begins to ask itself, 'who am I?', as it is physically and emotionally metamorphosing into something else.

In this adolescent phase, we can see most clearly the conflict created by the influence of different and competing peer groups.

Again, this will be further discussed in the next section.

It is also the moment when the adolescent has the means to break out of the energy fields that he has lived in for most of his life.

This is the moment when the projected fields of the parental figures are most challenged.

The outcome is a new, redefined set of identity fields.

But growth and change continue and the move from child, student to young adult, independent worker or 'mature' student, presents the person with new situations and challenges. Each bringing new opportunities for more changes.

As with serious relationships, academic and professional advances, marriage, children, etc., etc., life continues. And as we confront more and different situations, and so we continue to grow and to change.

So, to answer this part of the question of 'who am I?'

The answer is; 'someone different at every moment of your life'.

We grow and change through every contact and every situation that we experience.

Every person that we meet sees us differently and every one of these images influences how they treat us.

Every reaction of others then influences how we see ourselves, which in turn changes the way we act and react.

In short, they influence our identity fields.

14.6 The identity field

The identity field is the term that we use to describe the attitudes, behaviours, actions, reactions, image and self-image that a person expresses in any moment.

The basic premise of our model is, (unlike that of Rupert Sheldrake), that the components of any field can change at any moment and the fields are constructed and re-constructed continually.

That doesn't mean that many fields don't have a certain number of basic elements that are generally constant and are unlikely to change.

A very simplified image might be that of a person; their naked body can change, by growing older, or fatter or thinner, but in the very short term, the body does not change.

However, hair grows relatively quickly, one can have one's hair long or short, or coloured or in a pony-tail, plaited, or loose or pinned. The same that a man can be clean shaven, moustached, bearded, with or without sideburns.

And at any moment, one can choose to dress in any style that seems appropriate for the social – professional situation and the weather.

By the same logic; there are parts of the field that are almost totally fixed, (our sense of belonging to our families, society, country, religion), parts that can more easily change; (our social and peer groups, educational and professional situations), and then there are things that change all the time, (our moods, the people that we are with, desires of the moment).

The effect that the immediate environment can have on someone can range from close to zero, where the person is particularly insensible to outside influences, through to an almost total chameleon type transformation.

I remember meeting the teacher of a friend, whom I thought was exceptional, as he seemed to think exactly like me. It was only after he left, and I got the chance to talk to that friend that I found out that almost everyone ends up with same impression!

Depending on the environment, our inner state and how we see ourselves, our identity field can change almost constantly.

Often one of the most interesting yet uncomfortable experience for a teenager is when he and his friends meet his parents.

As he usually expresses one type of identity construction with his friends which can be particularly different from that with his parents. To watch him trying to 'be' a teen and a child at the same time, can be both amusing and instructive.

This field clearly demonstrates how, within a limited set of parameters, the active contents can combine and recombine, continually, to create an ever changing reality.

I remember clearly the headmaster of my school that could be screaming at us kids; red faced, full of violence, turning to one of 'his' teachers and talking in a quiet and relaxed tone. Only to turn and continue screaming at us.

We are all capable to present and express ourselves differently with different people, in different situations, based on different life events.

How useful and / or appropriate these different aspects of ourselves are or might be, will be reflected in later volumes.

15. Final thoughts on Volume 1

This first volume has set out to introduce you to the ideas and concepts behind the 'picturing the mind', model of us, we, human beings.

I have tried to follow the human process from conception through to some level of maturation, so as to demonstrate how the model can take into account the steps that we all see. Although not all will interpret these stages the same way.

If you have any thoughts, comments or criticisms, or desire to collaborate in any further elaboration of the concept, my private e-mail address is

gary.gedall@bluewin.ch.

Gentle reader, thank you for downloading this book and I very much hope that you have enjoyed it.

If so, please help others to make the choice to read this by sharing your views with your friends and writing a review on Amazon.

Thank you,

Kindest regards

Gary

Other works

By

Gary Edward Gedall

Picturing the Mind
Vol 2

The second volume following on from the initial concepts will reflect on such subjects as:

Relationships
Exchanging energy
Heart & Soul
Recuperation
Subjective constructions
An unconscious yes, an unconscious no
Me, myself and everyone else
Circles in circles, the micro level
Circles in circles, the macro level
Intuition
Metaphysical reflections

Picturing the Mind

Vol 3

Will deal with:

Psychopathology

Traditional psychotherapy
&
Alternative therapeutic approaches.

Island of Serenity Book 1
The Island of Survival

Pierre-Alain James 'Faron' Ferguson is about to commit suicide, in his suicide note he attempts to understand how he has come to have wrecked not only his own life, but also all of those around him.

Pierre-Alain James 'Faron' Ferguson finds himself in a type of 'no-mans-land', between here and there, he must accept to visit the 7 islands before he will be allowed to continue on to his next steps. The islands are named; Survival, Pleasure, Esteem, Love, Expression, Insight and lastly, the Island of Serenity

The Early Years:
Pierre-Alain James 'Faron' Ferguson is born into a well-to-do household of a factory owner, Scottish father and mother of a noble French family

He, and his younger brother Jay, grow up in a home of two distant but invested parents. Already, the first, small stones of his future problems are being put into place.

The Island of Survival:
Faron finds himself on the first of the seven islands, transformed into a prehistoric human form, he must learn how to interact with the local environment and the early humanoid tribe.

Here, he must reconnect with his instinct of survival.

Island of Serenity Book 2
Sun & Rain

This is the second chapter of Faron's life history, in which he falls in love, becomes a real cowboy, starts boarding school, finds his two best friends, and more than that would be telling too much.

FREE: If you have not yet read Book 1, Survival, no worries, I have included a shortened version, so as to introduce you to the story and the main characters.

Island of Serenity Book 3 (Vol 1)
The Island of Pleasure
Parts 1 & 2

Part 1.

Faron finds himself in a past version of Venice, as the owner of an old but grand hotel that doubles as the meeting place for the wealthy men of the City and the high class escort girls that live in the establishment.

Faron can do anything that he likes without limitation or cost. Not only can he avail himself of the girls, but can eat and drink, without limit, but never suffer from a hangover, nor gain a gram.

So why has the enigmatic guide brought him here, and will his limitless access to life's offerings really bring him the pleasure that he is destined to experience?

Part 2.

Faron is transformed into an adolescent tom boy. In this more modern version of Venice, 'he' has just 7 days to be made into a high class escort girl. What does this experience and the intrigues of the other persons within his sphere, mean for him, on his continuing quest to understand, and to experience, Pleasure?

Island of Serenity Book 3 (Vol 2) The Island of Pleasure
Parts 3 & 4

Part 3.

Faron finds himself in the mystery of a long ago Japan.

Who is this sad, young man that he must help to find back his pleasure in life?

And how does he end up in the middle of a war that it is impossible for him to participate in?

Part 4.

Faron arrives in India; projected into past moments of a native, and profoundly experiencing the realities of the present, Faron finally integrates the concept of pleasure into his tortured soul.

Tasty Bites

(Series – published or in preproduction**)**

Face to Face   A young teacher asks to befriend an older colleague on Face Book, "I have a very delicate situation, for which I would appreciate your advice"

Free 2 Luv   The e-mail exchanges between; RichBitch, SecretLover, the mother, the bestie, and the lawyer, expose a complicated and surprising story

Heresy   An e-mail from a future controlled by the major pharmaceutical companies, "please do what you can to change this situation, now, before it happens …

Love you to death   A toy town parable, populated by
                       your favourite playthings, about
                       the dangerous game of dependency
                       and co-dependency

Master of all Masters   In an ancient land, the
                           disciples argue about who is the
                           Master of all Masters. The solution
                           is to create a competition

Pandora's Box   If you had a magic box, into
                     which you could bury all your
                     negative thoughts and feelings,
                     wouldn't that be wonderful?

Shame of a family   Being born different can be a
                       heavy burden to bear.
                        Especially for the family

The Noble Princess   If you were just a humble Saxon,
                        would you be good enough to
                        marry a noble Norman Princess?

The Ugly Barren Fruit Tree   A weird foreign tree that bears no fruit, in an apple orchard. What value can it possibly have?

The Woman of my Dreams   What would you do, if the woman that you fell in love with in your dream, suddenly appears in real life?

The Zen approach to Low Impact Training and Sports
A simple method for achieving a healthy body and a healthy mind

Many of us approach our fitness and sports activities in an aggressive and competitive fashion.

And even if we feel that we succeed to break out of our comfort zones and win against ourselves or our opponent, there is an important cost to bear.

This level of violence that we have come to accept, so as to reach our goals is also an aggression against ourselves. By removing this need to 'win at any price', and tuning in with our bodies and emotions, we can achieve an enormous amount, all the while being in harmony with our mind, body and spirit.

The Zen approach to Low Impact Training and Sports, is a new softer approach where you can have the best of all worlds.

Adventures with the Master

Dhargey was a sickly child or so his parents treated him.
He was too weak to join the army or work in the fields or even join the monastery as a normal trainee monk.

To explain to the 'Young Master' why he should be accepted into the order with a lightened program, he was forced to accompany the revered old man a little ways up the mountain.

As his parents watched him leave; somewhere they felt that they would never see their sickly, fragile boy ever again, somewhere they were totally right.

He was a happy, healthy seven year old until he witnessed the riders, dressed in red and black, destroying his village and murdering his parents; the trauma cut deep into his psyche.

Only the chance meeting with a wandering monk could set him back onto the road towards health and serenity.

Through meditation, initiations, stories, taming wild horses, becoming a monkey, mastering the staff and the sword; the future 'Young Master' prepares to face his greatest demon.

Two men, two journeys, one goal.

REMEMBER

Stories and poems for self-help and self-development based on techniques of Ericksonian and auto-hypnosis

Dusk falls, the world shrinks little by little into a smaller and smaller circle as the light continues to diminish.
The centre of this world is illuminated by a small, crackling sun; the flames dance, and the rough faces of the people gathered there are lit by the fire of their expectations.
The old man will begin to speak, he will explain to them how the world is, how it was, how it was created. He will help them understand how things have a sense, an order, a way that they need to be.
He will clarify the sources of un-wellness and unhappiness, what is sickness, where it comes from, how to notice it and... how to heal it.
To heal the sick, he will call forth the forces of the invisible realms, maybe he will sing, certainly he will talk, and talk, and talk.

Since the beginning of time we have gathered round those who can bring us the answers to our questions and the means to alleviate our sufferings. This practice has not fundamentally changed since the earliest times; in every era, continent and culture we have found and continue to find these experiences.

In this, amongst the oldest of the healing traditions, he has succeeded to meld modern therapy theories and techniques with stories and poems of the highest quality.

With much humanity, clinical vignettes, common sense and lots of humour, the reader is gently carried from situation to situation. Whether the problems described concern you directly, indirectly or not at all, you will surely find interest and benefits from the wealth of insights and advices contained within and the conscious or unconscious positive changes through reading the stories and poems.

Lightning Source UK Ltd.
Milton Keynes UK
UKOW06f1913191215

265044UK00008B/76/P